Comments from class attendees:

"I felt love around, everywhere ... you could do this all the time!"

"I just want to let you know how much I appreciate the walk a few weeks ago. Your technique really helps me focus in the moment and surrender worries ... Your website led me to the book you wrote. ... Thank you!"

Reviews from previous Love Breathing book:

"I love this book – it is so easy to keep God in your mind when you practice love breathing – during a hectic day there is always time to breathe and focus. Thank you, this added another blessing to my life."

"Thanks for such a beautiful book."

'Love Breathing' is a sweet and practical guide to practicing the presence of God, yet taking it a step further, to the practice of 'loving' God, in every moment of daily life. Finding God is actually simple. It is we who make it so complicated. In this little pamphlet you'll find a guide to the spiritual simplicity of 'suffer the little children to come unto me, for such is the kingdom of God.'

— **Nayaswami Kriyananda,** author and founder
of the Ananda Self-Realization Communities

This book springs from the heart of actual experience and for that reason has unique power both to inspire and guide. It is simple, creative, and effective.

— **Asha Nayaswami,** author and Spiritual Director

"Thank you ... I could not stop reading ... an answer to my prayer, ... you spoke to my heart through your book."

"Wow! ... I am going to start practicing!"

The daily practice of "love breathing" will transform your life for the better.

—**Helen Purcell,** Director of Living Wisdom School

The partially blossomed, partially budded yellow rose on the cover symbolizes a heart starting to open to God. The inner budded portion is still closed and hasn't completely given itself over to God. The outer petals have opened to both receive and radiate God's love.

Love Breathing Walking Meditation

Eric Munro

Contents

Expanded Discussions

Several topics are discussed in more depth here.

A stream of consciousness monologue relating what happens during a fairly typical walking meditation for the author.

If you are new to meditation or have found sitting meditations difficult, read this section before the training manual.

Introduction

Many people take walks to clear their minds, feel more at peace, become more invigorated, think about problems, receive inspiration, ... Indeed, just the act of walking inherently benefits people on many levels: physically, emotionally, mentally, and spiritually.

Using walks as a tool for spiritual development though is largely untapped in the world today. Yet a vast reservoir of potential awaits any spiritual seeker who chooses to utilize this wonderful tool.

A love breathing walking meditation offers a reliable, repeatable routine for experiencing a joyful, loving communion with the Divine, with God, with each walk taken.

It is a technique I have been practicing and exploring for over a decade now. It still amazes me that it doesn't matter if I start a walk when extremely distracted or even extremely upset. Without fail, after walking for 30 minutes while following the routine, I end up in a joyful, uplifted state.

This book starts with some personal experiences and what led me to this practice. Then comes a "training manual" one can use for self-paced learning. Followed by a section with more in-depth discussion. At the end, a stream of consciousness monologue goes over what a typical walking meditation is like for myself.

Some people after reading the monologue have commented, "this seems very hard."

It is not. While it does take focused effort, it does not require some all-out brute force exertion. Indeed, trying to hard prevents one from going deep into a divine communion. Instead, there is a coaxing process that invites the Divine in slowly at first, then more and more. The Divine does the real work! We just need to intelligently coax the Divine in. A unique coaxing process is offered here. When mastered, one can repeatably coax oneself into a joyful, peaceful space.

Practicing walking meditation also helps one keep a spiritual connection alive through the normal activities of an active day. Through the practice, one becomes proficient in keeping a spiritual connection alive while walking and with eyes open. The same techniques can be used to open a spiritual connection while driving, shopping, cooking, cleaning, washing dishes, writing, gardening, attending meetings, zooming, ...

Both beginning and experienced meditators can utilize these techniques. I had been meditating for over 15 years before starting walking meditations. The walks help me go quite deeply into communion and my focus, especially at the end of a walk, becomes quite intense. After a walk, I sit and have my deepest sitting meditations then.

For a beginner, the intense focus would probably turn someone off from even trying. Gracefully though, one can simply apply the coaxing methods to the extent that is helpful for them.

I found it unwieldy to try and write the training manual for both beginning and experienced meditators. So the training manual mirrors my own experience and thus is targeted more towards people experienced in meditation. For beginners, please first read the section at the end for beginners.

Also, if your spiritual perceptions don't include the word God, don't let the use of the word turn you away. Just substitute whatever word or phrase means an all-loving, all-conscious force to you.

with joyful blessings,
Eric Munro

By the practice of meditation,
you will find that you are carrying within
your heart a portable paradise.

—Paramhansa Yogananda

Spheres of Ecstasy

"See you soon."

"Bye Dad."

I had just dropped off my younger, 11-year-old son, at Living Wisdom School. In a little less than an hour I needed to return and help out as a volunteer in the middle school math class. Rushing, I drive to a nearby park, exit the car and start walking with exuberant expectation.

The crisp fall air invigorated with its fresh post-rain aroma. A few white fluffy clouds floated happily across the blue morning sky. They welcomed me as I my tennis shoes met the sidewalk across the street from my car. Down this tree-lined suburban street a few people were already enjoying walks, some with their dogs on line.

"Maybe today someone will ask me where all this joy comes from and I can show them this way to access it."

"The nature of joy is to expand, to be shared," is a wonderfully accurate quote, one which continues to hound me.

Walking on, I choose a north-south direction so the low early morning sun will not blind my eyes. It's only been a month since I started these walks and my inner life has been totally transformed, indeed the prison cell my spirit inhabited was shattering in explosions of ecstasy.

Hustling while looking at my watch, "30 minutes to walk leaves 20 minutes to sit in my car meditating before I need to return to the school." With excited impatience, I start practicing this recently revealed 'love breathing.' After about 15 minutes, like clockwork, the calm tingling permeates throughout my body. A sparkling joy arises in my heart all the way up through my head out to God above. In my mind's eye, a loving, brilliant white light shines down on me. "Thank you God, thank you Gurus." God's love; so sweet, sweeter than the finest vanilla ice cream; so palpable, more palpable than the autumn breeze blowing across my skin.

Walking past a pedestrian in this state of bliss, I smile and wonder will he ask me about this? He doesn't and I walk on. Walking slowly, very slowly, so I can wholly savor this sacred communion, I return to my car. It is a simple box shaped car with a high roof. With providence, I purchased it years earlier so I could sit upright in it while meditating during lunch breaks. Or now, after a love breathing walk.

The car was parked under a tall Monterey Pine tree which had overgrown its normal size in this protected Bay Area, California climate. I climbed in. It was parked with the driver's seat along the park green, away from the road, making the sounds of passing cars less distracting. Some pedestrians would walk by on the park path alongside my car while I meditated. Previously this left me feeling self-conscious. Not now, it didn't matter. The Divine nectar's allure subdued all such concerns. Sitting straight with spine erect, I closed my eyes in meditation. After a brief few minutes, it started again.

Inwardly at the base of my spine, I saw and felt a shimmering sphere whose surface comprised of thousands of clear, small diamond-like crystals. A brilliant white and golden light shined through and all around the sphere. The sphere rose up my spine into my head. It exploded in a flash of rapturous ecstasy. An ecstasy so intense that every earthly pleasure seemed but a dull, muddy sensation in comparison.

Then another sphere formed at my spine's base. It rose and it too exploded in ecstasy.

Another one formed, rose, exploded.

And another ... and another ....

After a few short minutes of this which seemed to last for an extended eternity, the spheres stopped. I continued in joyous meditation while first quickly checking my watch. I wanted desperately to stay in prolonged silent meditation, but I had made a commitment to help out with math class. So, after a few more minutes I drove off, thinking "well, I can do this again tomorrow." For a couple weeks it did continue, not every day, but about every other day. Since then, however, for the past 12 years, it has not repeated.

While the rapturous intensity of those couple weeks has not returned, what remains, or more accurately stated, what has been developed, is a wonderful, inner, sparkling joy. A joy accessible within a few breaths, if I so choose.

The quest for this sparkling joy emerged early in my youth. Against a backdrop of childhood sullenness, a few of its sparks came through, enticing a lifelong search.

Comment on peak spiritual or superconscious experiences

It is my hope, by sharing some of my own superconscious experiences in this book, it will inspire others along in their own spiritual journey, to encourage others to try these spiritual practices and see if they can benefit from them. The plethora of spiritual practices in the world seems endless and probably is. Every individual must find the ones most attuned to their nature, most personally helpful.

Whether we label them superconscious or not, God gives everyone experiences outside their normal "state of consciousness." These gifts from God, however fleeting, are meant to show us what lies ahead, meant to inspire us upward.

Sometimes though, many times probably, they can be a source of frustration and even cause us to turn away from spiritual efforts. Hearing about someone else's experience or even remembering one's own experience can cause painful frustration. One thinks, "I can't, I don't experience that," or "I only felt that once and no matter how hard

I try, I can't feel it again." The danger is one forgets the spiritual search to avoid the pain of frustration.

This happened in my own life after having some experiences in early youth. Unable to "recreate" them, I forgot about the spiritual search for decades.

Our spiritual efforts may not take us to superconsciousness on a timetable we desire. Our efforts will, though, get us closer and increase love and joy in our day-to-day lives. Ultimately, but not necessarily in this one lifetime, we will arrive and live in unity in God.

Finding the trailhead

"Hurry up kids and come down for breakfast, we must leave for church soon" our mother beckoned to us six children, all in various states of getting out of bed and getting dressed. Lumbering downstairs, we sat on the long wooden benches on either side of our large and only eating table.

"Eat quickly and come get into the car" our father called out as he went outside to start up the large station wagon. He moved it to right outside the front door with the motor running, all to expedite loading up the family.

Sunday mornings were a strange time. The chaotic stress of getting us up, fed, and out to the car in time, left me feeling less than uplifted. But then getting to church, everyone, children and adults together gathered in the main room. The air started to sparkle with joy as everyone started singing together:

...

That greetings glorious from high heaven,
Whence joys supernal flow,
Come from that Love, divinely near,
Which chastens pride and earth-born fear,

...

'Twas Love whose finger traced aloud
A bow of promise on the cloud.

...

Whether people sang in tune or not, the sweetness of the music melted away all the tension of getting there ... made it all worthwhile. After the song ends, Sunday School teachers corral us downstairs into a basement room outfitted with large round tables for the various classes.

An older woman this Sunday leads my class. "Did you all read the lesson this week?" "Let's go over a few parts of it in class."

After several minutes of strained conversation, my thoughts observe "this teacher really has no idea how to make this interesting to us, ... it is nice she is trying, too bad she's struggling so and feeling uncomfortable ... How could this be interesting? ... I don't have any idea myself how it could be made interesting ... Guess we both just need to suffer through this hour together."

Knock, knock, knock, the door to our classroom opens, a man interrupts, "it's time to go upstairs for the last hymn, hurry or you will miss it." Like coiled springs being released, we all jump up, run upstairs.

Saw ye my Saviour? Heard ye the glad sound?
Felt ye the power of the Word?
'Twas the Truth that made us free,
And was found by you and me
In the life and the love of our Lord.
...

The sparkling joy returns, filling the room, everyone was happy. The joy lingers while people converse after church, into the parking lot, until we all load into our cars. Sitting in the back seat while being driven home, thoughts enter:

"Why doesn't the sparkling joy continue? Making it continue is what I want to learn in Sunday school."

Singing hymns at church, were my first recollections that a divine, sparkling joy exists. Consciously and unconsciously they prompted a lifelong search for it.

Another significant recollection punctuates my childhood.

My mother considered me somewhat troubled as a youth. For me, being a moody introvert seemed like a natural state of being. Many times, playing alone in the woods felt magical. A soft bed of decaying leaves to walk on, the crisp air with an aroma of freshly rained on soil, silent trees smiled as I passed by. A gurgling brook provided hours of entertainment for me to build dams in, walk in, or just to sit along its edge. Sometimes loneliness morphed into internal anger and I would run through the woods whacking away at dead tree limbs in rage, not even knowing where the anger came from.

In an attempt to help me, once as a pre-teen, my mother brought me to see Auntie Kim, a Christian Science Practitioner, a spiritual healer in our church. Auntie Kim radiated a wonderful aura of Godly, motherly love. She was well known in our church circles as having affected many miraculous healings. While my mother drove me to her house, over an hour away, I sat watching the scenery. Mostly trees adorned these small roads in rural, northern New Hampshire. Interspersed with forests where some homes, little towns and many lakes. I felt uncomfortable about this intervention, this intrusion, into my personal private space. Yet at the same time, I felt somewhat hopeful, "maybe this could make a difference, could find out how to be happier, feel the divine."

Arriving at Auntie Kim's front door, she welcomed us, "Hello, so good to see you, come in." Walking in she directed me; "Eric, why don't you sit here in the living room first, while your mother and I talk for a moment, OK?"

"OK." My mother and Auntie Kim went into another room to converse.

A large stone fireplace added a solidness, a foundation to the entire living room. Looking at it left you feeling calm, at peace. Next to the fireplace, I sat at one end of a white plush couch. The kind of couch where you sink into the cushions while they rise up around you, coddling you. The couch mirrored Auntie Kim's aura of motherly, embracing love. She entered the room and sat across from me on the other side of the couch, love energy expanded from her in an unseen, yet palpable wave. Her eyes shined like warm, sweet crystals in the sun. "How are you doing Eric."

"OK."

She proceeded to ask me a few questions, trying to get me to talk. Mostly though, I remained in stoic silence, maybe offering a one-word answer now and then. My mind though was in overdrive:

"Auntie Kim really has what I want, that God connection, that sparking joy … maybe I should open up to her, maybe I can learn it from her … go on, just talk to her."

But in a moment of clear, self-awareness that startled me, I thought:

"but I can't, her motherly love is just too much, I'm an older boy, I need to get away from this motherliness to grow. It was ok when I was younger, now it's suffocating. Maybe I could open up to a man, too bad we don't know any male Christian Science Practitioners who have Auntie Kim's divine connection."

Auntie Kim informed my mother there was nothing she could do if I didn't open up. We left. Feeling quite remorseful, quite despondent in the car, staring at trees going by on the drive home, I contemplated: "well that's how it needs to be, grow up on my own, maybe someday I can find a way to that God connection."

Although that short interchange didn't result in anything tangible at the time, I am eternally grateful for it. My mother probably never realized what an impact it had on me. Indian scriptures have a saying: "One moment in the company of a saint can be your raft over the ocean of delusion." Being in Auntie Kim's presence just for that short time, helped keep burning in me a long simmering desire for God, for the divine, sparkling joy.

In the ensuing years, I mostly gave up thinking about God, since no practical way to connect with Him presented itself. From time to time I would read the Bible and Science & Health, a Christian Science book. Silently singing hymns to myself provided occasional inspiration.

Through high school, through college, my attention shifted to relationships, career and all the usual interests of youth growing into adulthood. Our family moved my freshman year of high school to another small town in the neighboring state of Maine. I enjoyed math and focused on it at this new school. Becoming the top math team member and winning the state tournament one year, helped get me admitted to M.I.T for college. After college, with an electrical engineering degree, I moved to the Bay Area of California for work.

Caught up in all the changes and new experiences life kept offering, spiritual yearnings only kept smoldering, not igniting.

A friend recommended a workshop to me, one of those pseudo-spiritual, personal growth workshops that were popular in the early 1980s. It was an eye-opener, revealing an expanded field of spiritual pursuits I never knew existed outside my traditional church upbringing. It also introduced me to meditation, indeed it was my first exposure to the word "meditation." They did an exercise meant to show you how self-critical you were. It succeeded wonderfully leaving many participants, myself included, feeling "why am I so upset over such a trivial thing, so I failed to write within the journal margins they proscribed, big deal?" After this unsettling exercise they had us meditate. "Close your eyes, breathe deeply and just listen to your breath." Closing my eyes, I quickly transported from agitation to calmness. A peace descended on me with a deep sense everything is OK. A stillness seemingly stopped every atom in my body from vibrating. Awake, yet unaware of the outside world. After being called out of the meditation, I thought "wow, what was that! I need to find out more."

Starting then, I looked into different meditation techniques, different spiritual groups, did a lot of reading, frequenting the local spiritual bookshops. Attended a workshop given by Brugh Joy, a spiritual teacher. In him I saw again the divine radiance I had seen in Auntie Kim over a decade prior. I really tried to practice the "spiral chakra meditation" he taught, basically energizing the chakras in a spiral pattern out from the heart. It worked somewhat, but proved frustrating. I would start doing it and then go into a meditative state where, if I kept focusing on energizing the chakras it would take me out of the meditative state. But if I stopped focusing on the chakras, I could hold the meditative state only for a bit, but not for long as random thoughts entered and took me out. Quite frustrating, being able to get a little taste of meditative joy, but no way for me to hold on to it for an extended time.

I joined and fell out of other spiritual groups and endeavors over the next decade. A decade where I went to graduate school, getting an MBA. Secured a career in executive management at a fast-growing semiconductor firm. Married, had two sons.

In this decade, I spent a few months in a spiritual group headed by a man who had split off from Eckankar. Learned their meditation technique, which basically focused your attention at the spiritual eye and beyond. Whereas the spiral meditation proved mentally too complex for me, this technique proved too simple. My mind would go off on random thoughts too easily. Maybe with great discipline and practice, this technique would have been useful long term for me, but I lacked the discipline to try it for more than a few months.

For a few years I withdrew from being part of any spiritual group, or even going to any spiritual event or class. After marrying and settling into a long-term career my life stabilized. The previous constant changes around education, work, and relationships subsided into a routine life. It was then I decided "I need a strong spiritual group to join, all the progress I've made so far has been when I was part of a group."

So with methodical efficiency I started visiting different groups in the area, on a kind of shopping-spree search for the best spiritual group for myself. I ended up attending a Sunday service at Ananda Palo Alto, carefully sitting in the back of the long rectangular office building room they rented for their church at the time. The chanting enthralled, like singing hymns during childhood. After the service, I stood off in the background observing these people. "So many people with so much light in their eyes! … I've only encountered this kind of light in Auntie Kim's and Brugh Joy's eyes before … here is a room full of such people! … I want what they have." I made Ananda my spiritual home, for over 25 years now.

Quickly I took the basic meditation course they taught. My engineering mindset marveled at its simplicity and comparative wondrous effectiveness. The technique, called Hong Sau, used similar elements I had learned elsewhere, breathing, chakra energization, mantra. Yet they put the elements together in a way which made it much easier, still not easy, but much easier to meditate. It wasn't too complex, so the mental focus required didn't prevent you from entering and staying in a meditative state. Yet it wasn't too simple, so random thoughts didn't get a free pass into your mind. Such an inspired meditative engineering design!

For the next 15 years, I meditated regularly, served, volunteered, donated to Ananda as able, given I had a young family and demanding career. I was on a solid path, making spiritual progress. Yet an underlying quiet desperation remained. At times, during meditations, during church services, or just serving with members, I could feel a deep inner connection and experience the sparkling joy, but only sporadically. It felt like swimming in river rapids that pushed you underwater most of the time. Struggling, desperate for air you come up from time to time to gasp, only to be submerged again. Adding to the frustration, you can see others sitting on the riverbanks enjoying the sparkling joy, breathing the air you so desperately want.

My career engaged, stimulated, challenged and rewarded financially. The company grew rapidly during the 1990s high tech bubble. Everyone there, myself included, reveled in the wealth we were creating for ourselves and we all worked hard together to keep it coming. Yet after a few years I started to pray to be released from it. Being in a group of people where money was the main motivation, main topic of discussion, wore away at me. Every quarter, we had a Directors' offsite meeting. The directors or VPs of certain groups presented to everyone their future plans for their business units or how they were continuing to improve their departments. I started sitting in the back. The overwhelming aura of ego driven, money motivated desire and fear mixed together in what felt to be a noxious gas that burned away at my soul joy. I attribute my budding meditation practice for this turn of attitude.

My company built a new office building. It was a marvel of ego stroking architecture. A normal rectangular building has four corners, this one had over a dozen corners. So, on every floor you could have more than a dozen corner offices for executives. When my turn came to pick an office, I choose a small corner office which had trees outside. A manager asked "why are picking that small office and not the large one over here? If you don't want it, can I?"

"Sure, no problem." The small office, without windows to the inner hallways, offered a cloistered feel, and with the door shut I could go inward, even meditate briefly on company time. Many times in this office, I prayed to be released.

Interestingly, after I finally internally accepted that maybe God wanted me to stay here, maybe just serving this way is enough this lifetime, it was then I was released. In 2008, my business unit went through a downsizing. I could stay and head a unit that would be "milked," i.e. not invested in any more, but kept going as long as it generated profits. For a very short time I looked for opportunities at other companies, but my heart flatlined whenever a possible opportunity arose. I thought of leaving professional career life. Running through the numbers of my finances, I saw my family could be provided for without my working. Sitting then in my office, seriously contemplating whether to leave or stay, I heard a strong, inner divine voice say:

"You'd be absolutely insane to stay where you are."

Inwardly I laughed, felt relieved and grateful. God, like a teasing friend, had just given me permission to leave without looking back or second-guessing myself. I quit my career.

What relief! No more high intensity, pressure filled job. No more worrying about your business unit sales. No more trying to please the CEO. No more placating irate customers not getting their parts in time. No more running ragged to get everything done. I could do anything with my days or nothing with my days.

The year after this release proved the hardest of my life. I in fact had nothing to do! Didn't know what to do. My previous self-identity as a successful executive ... gone. Indeed doing nothing proved much more stressful than having a high-stress job.

To keep somewhat active, I volunteered at my sons' school, Living Wisdom School. Helped out with marketing and answering math questions for middle-school-aged children. I wanted to make spiritual progress ... fast. The high-tech work culture doesn't acknowledge patience as a virtue, this impatience learned, added to my frustration. I had quit to make spiritual progress, yet it wasn't happening.

Much of my time was spent chauffeuring my sons around and waiting for them at school or some after-school activity. During these waiting periods, I had been trying different spiritual activities. I tried meditating in my car, but I didn't feel enough inspiration and couldn't will myself to continue this. I practiced japa, the Indian technique of constantly repeating God's name. I became very good at silently saying "God" while also feeling upset that I didn't feel joy! Having been inspired by Frank Laubach's and Brother Lawrence's Practicing the Presence of God methods, I tried thinking about God and talking with God while sitting at parks and taking walks. Some fleeting inspirations came; they weren't enough, and I quit trying. I finally gave up that first year and just sank into reading the newspaper, internet surfing, and doing random household chores.

At the start of the next school year, I had dropped my sons off at school, drove to a nearby park and sat inside my car. Feeling utterly despondent, I thought about getting coffee and reading the newspaper; instead, though, I felt, "No, I can't repeat this anymore."

Pleading with God through tears, "God it's been over a year, what should I do? ... I have been trying everything, what should I do? ... I don't know what to do ... the best thing I've tried this last year is taking walks, they haven't been great, but they are the best I can think of ... OK then God, I'll continue to take walks ... it's the best I know how to do."

Getting out of the car, I walked across the road into a tree-lined residential area. As soon as my foot hit the sidewalk, I saw a flash of golden light coming from in back of my head on my right side. Simultaneously, a loud voice, unmistakably that of my chosen Guru, commanded me:

"Love God! God wants your love! God needs your love! Love Him!"

My whole body electrified, despair disappeared, joyful exuberance exploded all around me. My thoughts reeled:

"Of course, I've been meditating, serving, but loving God, the most important commandment by the way, is just a mental concept to me. I've thought about loving God, had a concept of loving God, but I've never really practiced loving God, not with my heart ... how dense of me! ... I need to practice loving God! ... How do I practice loving God? ... Well, this revelation came to me when taking a walk, so I'll practice loving God while taking a walk!"

With that I started walking and thinking *"how can I do this?"*

This started what I now call love breathing, walking meditations.

This day was the key pivot point of my life.

The day my Guru ordered me:

"Love God!"

The Exploration

The next several weeks, for me, were an exhilarated high of joyous, expectant exploration.

On that first, fateful walk I thought: *"this is it ... it is really going to happen this time ... the doorway I need will be found ... and soon!"*

With a calm absolute knowing it would happen, I decided to find the best method for myself to practice loving God while taking a walk, to optimize a technique for reliably entering into a joyous, loving communion with God while taking a walk. The basic method came in only a couple weeks, the optimization continues today for me over 10 years later.

It was a wonderful engaging challenge; how to stay energized and focused on loving God despite the internal onslaught of random thoughts and emotions.

Fortunately staying energetic wasn't really an obstacle. Walking naturally kept my energy elevated. However, optimization tradeoffs abounded when addressing the random thought and emotion obstacles. For instance, mentally repeating the Lord's Prayer or the Gayatri Mantra would help keep random thoughts at bay. But it took so much mental focus to keep repeating them, I couldn't then focus on sending God my love energy. Trying to direct energy through the chakras, like is done in Hong Sau or other meditations, also proved too complicated. It took so much mental focus to do this while walking at the same time, I had no focus left for loving God.

A technique was needed that wasn't too complicated or my total focus would be on doing the technique, not loving God. But there had to be some technique to help focus my thoughts, emotions, energy to loving God. Otherwise, random mundane thoughts and emotions would overwhelm and derail me from loving God.

I knew from my experience of trying out many different meditation techniques, that even a slight difference in methods can yield much different results. My thought was, "let's try out all the spiritual techniques I know, let's try rearranging them in different combinations, to find the best one to help me love God while walking."

Every morning after dropping my sons off at school, I went for a walk trying out new methods. Then after helping out with math class at the school, I'd go for another walk, trying something else. I felt like a kid in a 31 flavors ice cream store, sampling different flavor combinations to find that one, most delectable combination.

… different breathing techniques … listening to chants … listening to hymns … energizing heart chakra … sending God love from the heart … synchronize to the breath … look up … look down … look sideways … walk fast … walk slow … walk normal … breathe very deeply … don't breathe (didn't work) … do hong sau while walking … do Kriya Yoga meditation while walking … silently chant … do mantra "I love you God" … … … … … …"

I tried just sending God love out from my heart chakra, very difficult to sustain. So, I then tried sending out love, only on the out-breath, easier to sustain, but still difficult and didn't really end up feeling very uplifting. One night, while thinking about what to try the next day, I reasoned, "obviously I should try to receive and send love from my heart, the love center, but this didn't feel

28

uplifting. Well, we have been taught to keep our consciousness uplifted at the spiritual eye center, so maybe I need to incorporate the spiritual eye chakra in this practice. So I'll try breathing in love from God into my spiritual eye, then I'll breath that love back out to God through the heart."

That night, with notable anticipation for the next day, I felt; "this could be it; this is getting really close."

The next day, the next morning, I started my walk with heighten hope, "this could be it."

Breathing in God's love into the spiritual eye, breathing out love from the heart. In ... out ... in ... out ... After a few minutes of this, it felt awful. Not uplifting at all, in fact, actively downlifting, like I was trying to force the love energy in an unnatural, constrictive direction. Continuing walking I thought, "oh well, that doesn't work ... still there is something here ... I know it ... what else ... maybe if I just flip the energy flow around, have it go in the other direction."

Upon doing this, I felt uplifted, each breath became more uplifting. I sensed the calm, distinct, silent presence of my Guru behind off to the side of me. An inner knowing came from Him, "this is it, this is the basic technique, other refinements, other optimizations will come, but this is the basic technique."

Inwardly rejoicing with overflowing, overwhelming gratitude I kept walking.

Finally, at 47 years 2 months of age,
in September 2009,
the door I needed was opened.

Everyone must find their own way

to make love to God.

– Paramhansa Yogananda

Everyone would benefit from including a daily practice of loving God. A good question to ask oneself is "how do I practice loving God each day." If no obvious, simple answer comes, start a practice right away! Make it a real practice of the heart, not a mental concept or mental ritual as I had done. As everyone is unique, people will have unique "loving God practices." Since we are, though, "cut from the same cloth," this love breathing walking meditation is offered to anyone who might benefit from it, anyone who shares a similar cloth in God.

Master on the hill

*A meditation shared while
sitting in Sunday service*

About a year after starting the walking meditations, a vivid meditation came while sitting during church. I had been taking walking meditations before church at this time as a way to help go deep into the inspiration Sunday services offered.

Sitting with eyes closed I had been listening to the choir, breathing in and out devotion to God, when vividly I saw in my inner gaze a grassy hillside directly in front. The long, green grass bent over, undulating in the breeze. The invigorating, cool, fresh crisp aroma of spring blew across the landscape. A smattering of white puff clouds decorated the sky-blue background above. The Master stood on the hilltop, looking down at me standing at the bottom of the hill.

Looking up longingly, I realized getting to the top of the hill represented enlightenment, total self-realization, being one with God. I desperately wanted to be up there with Master. Yet when looking and contemplating hiking up, I realized the hillside was a land mine field. Not knowing where the land mines were, I stood frozen in fear. Such unbearable anguish, wanting to run up, but too afraid to try, lest I be blown up.

Then Master, with a palpable aura of compassion, came down the hillside and outstretched his hand to mine. I reached out and held it dear. Master then turned back up and proceeded to lead me up the hillside. Such an overwhelming feeling of joyful relief blew over me. Master was going to lead me safely up the hillside to the top. He will lead me around all these land mines. Holding his hand, feeling Master's total compassion for me, he led me up to and over the closest land mine.

I blew up!

Then still holding my hand, he led me to the next closest land mine, and I blew up again! On to the next land mine ... step on it ... blow up! Then to the next, and the next, blowing up again over and over. With each explosion I felt and visualized the ego-shell around me, encasing my consciousness, would crack and a piece of it would fall off.

"Oh! ... Master is having me step on these land mines to help get rid of my ego!"

I realized by the time we reached the top of the hill; no ego shell would be left.

Inwardly I started laughing in sheer amusement at this ironic twist of expectations. I had been thinking, feeling safe that Master would lead me around the land mines, when in fact he led me to step on them!

The meditative vision ended in internal laughter.

This meditation happened over a decade ago, yet I still refer to it inwardly. Whenever something goes wrong in my life, when a project fails, or some outward expectation isn't met; I inwardly address Master;

OK another land mine blowing up ...
thank you Master ... I guess ... aum

God Space

A walking meditation recollection

The golden hour, the time right before sunset is known and cherished by farmers and others who spend time outside as daylight passes into twilight. A soft golden luminance emanates seemingly from everywhere, mixes with the green tinge of trees and plants, creating a magical tingling feeling of peaceful delight for anyone willing to slow down and breathe it in.

During such a golden hour in May 2018, a window opened briefly, allowing me to perceive a fragment of God's nature.

The back parking lot of the Ananda Community stretches for about four to five hundred feet. A tall row of towering Eucalyptus trees, with their wafting aroma, separates the lot from the adjoining railroad track. On the other side, a row of mature Carob trees separates the lot from the ageing 2-story apartment buildings. An almost perfect corridor is created for walking meditations. Large mature trees on either side, with a clear view of the sky down the middle. The sun doesn't blind, hiding behind the buildings close to sunset. The occasional distracting car provides a manageable challenge to keeps one's inner gaze on God. The less occasional train horn can totally distract or can shock one's energy higher while forcing a total focus on God. An exceptional training course to exercise inner communion.

Slightly before 8 p.m., I was on the last part of a walking meditation. Walking alone, I had just passed under a Carob tree when my outer vision ceased, and my normal self also ceased. An awareness of being all and only overtook my consciousness. Thoughts slowly entered;

> *"This is what God is ... this is what being God is ... interesting.*
> *Infinite peace ... infinite stillness ...*
> *infinite unmanifested potentiality. This was God."*

Yet while completely calm, a powerful energy pervaded everywhere; unutilized, in a state of stasis, waiting for a thought to direct it into action. It felt like being superheated water. Water can be heated above the boiling point without boiling. But then any perturbation, any movement will cause a cascade of boiling bubbles to erupt. The God-space felt like this, not the heat sensation, but the feeling any perturbation of thought would cause manifestation and a tumultuous exit from this God-space. Maybe this is the nothingness Buddhists refer to; thoughtless, all-aware, pure consciousness, from which everything and anything arises.

In the far distance of my inner gaze, the only gaze available to me at the time, was a plane of golden translucent glass. On the surface, a tiny mushroom cloud emerged, no bigger than a dime in my extended view. With it emerged the thought:

> *this is a new universe being created ... interesting.*

Then on my left side down by my feet, in back of me, I perceived a shadow. A small shadow that was fading. A realization entered;

> *this is my ego, it is not me, I am not it.*

As it continued to fade, another realization;

> *if I want to get back to this God-space, I must totally,*
> *<u>absolutely totally,</u> let this ego-shadow go.*

Then, as I tried to let the ego go, a sizeable fear was triggered and the experience ended.

I walked to the meditation room of the community and then while meditating, entered into this God-space again, but only for second. The next morning while waking, I again briefly felt the God-space. Since then, I have not felt it completely again. But it looms now as a beacon in my consciousness

> *... you know what is necessary, let the ego go,*
> *let it fade into just a memory.*

Freedom comes ... by attuning oneself deeply with the all-loving Inner Silence.

– Paramhansa Yogananda

Love Breathing

Walking Meditation

Training Manual

How to use this manual

This manual attempts to provide a step-by-step training for establishing and developing a walking meditation practice. The question naturally arises, why do this? what is the purpose? what is the goal?

Having a goal in mind, directs and focuses the practice. Indeed a "walking meditation" practice with the goal to burn calories and increase cardiovascular health would look very different than a practice with a more spiritual goal.

The goal this book revolves around is:

In a 30-minute walk, establish as deep an ecstatic communion with God as possible.

When starting a walk, what runs through my mind is:

"over the next 30 minutes how can I get as close as possible to God, to Infinite Bliss."

Naturally this is a directional, aspirational goal that guides the practice, where success is measured by the progress made from where one is starting, rather than how close one gets to Infinite Bliss!

It's recommended you spend about a week on each of the 14 sections. If you read cover to cover and practice all the techniques at once, it probably will not be very effective for you and could lead you to quit thinking, "this doesn't work for me." Indeed that was a problem when I first started sharing this with others and tried to do it too quickly or in just a one workshop or during a drop-in walking meditation. The coaxing process is key, and it takes time to work with oneself to master it. Once mastered, though, it will seem remarkable how relatively quickly and reliably one can enter into a satisfying divine communion.

Do go through the first 4 sections in order and spend more time on the coaxing section as needed. The later sections deal with specific issues that you may or may not relate to. At that point, you might want to skim the rest of the course and do the sections that make sense to you based on your own challenges. Also the discussion chapters go into more depth on various aspects of the practice. These have been separated from the 14-section course, so that the course text doesn't get too lengthy and each discussion topic can be more easily referenced. Read the discussion topics in any order desired.

You should try to walk at least 3 times a week for 30 minutes each time. Then if you already have a sitting meditation practice, sit to meditate after the walk, even if it is just for 10 minutes. Personally, I have my best sitting meditations right after a walking meditation. A walking meditation can bring up a lot of energy. Sitting quietly afterwards will help interiorize all that energy and strengthen your "spiritual core."

Finally, when learning you might consider starting a group to learn together. Find a few friends or colleagues who would be interested and then meet once a week for about 1.5 hours. A suggested format is:

0 to 30 minutes: Discussion of how everyone's individual practice went during the week and go over the next section to start trying at this meeting.

30 to 60 minutes: Do a walking meditation at the same time, but don't walk side-by-side. Stagger your walking or walk in different directions. Walking side-by-side makes it more difficult to focus on God.

60 to 90 minutes: Come back together and have a sitting meditation and/or a discussion or can also just go home in silence.

1. Starting Out

Many times, people seeking personal or spiritual growth will focus too much effort on improving themselves. The idea takes hold that they must fix a laundry list of their faults before they can experience any divine communion.

It's as if they are inside the "house" of their own being and trying to clean it up before they invite God inside. But God is "outside" their house banging on the doors and windows, asking to be let in. He doesn't care how dirty it is inside. He wants to come in. If we let Him, He will help clean up the mess with us. This is grace—letting God into your heart, and He then changes you.

How do we open the door to our house and heart to God? It's actually quite simple. Practice the greatest commandment: "Love God with all your heart ..."

God is wildly in love with you. He can't resist any love you give Him, and He cries when you ignore Him. If you want God by your side, send Him a little love. He can't resist it. He's like a child with no self-control being offered a candy. One love offering from you and God will immediately come to your side.

God is infinite consciousness, infinite bliss. Love is the great connecting force. Anything you love will be drawn closer to you. The answer to: "why practice loving God?" is very simple. Practice so you will be drawn closer to infinite bliss. Spend more time practicing loving infinity, less time loving finiteness.

Practice loving God every day. Make it a routine part of your life. Daily dedicate some fixed amount of time where you only practice loving God with feeling in your heart. Spend 80% of your spiritual efforts on loving God and 20% on fixing yourself. If you do this, communion with the divine will become a daily joy, and grace will start cleaning your "inner house."

Exercise 1: Before reading any further, go out alone and walk for 30 minutes. Ideally start walking right outside your residence. Dedicate the walk to God. Inwardly ask God at the start, "God, during this walk, how can I move closer to you, how can I open my heart and love you more, how can I feel your Presence." While walking; listen for God's response.

If you do this daily for the rest of your life, a wonderful walking practice of communing with God will emerge suited to your own individual nature.

While this exercise will most likely prove difficult, I recommend you do this for a week before reading on and trying the methods in this manual. Doing this first will help you develop a more personal, intimate relationship with God. The underlying intent of this love breathing, walking meditation is to develop an ongoing communion with God. For a genuine relationship, it is good to start by dedicating some time, with an open-ended intent, without following any rules or practicing any specific techniques.

2. Love Breathing technique

Right where you are, sit up straight, keep your head level, but look up slightly by lifting your eyes up, not your whole head. Ideally look around out a window or off into some distance, depending on where you are. Breathe a little more deeply than normal, but not so much you start feeling out of breath. When breathing in, feel love energy from all around come into your heart filling and energizing it. When breathing out feel love energy go out from your forehead (the spiritual eye chakra) to the point you are gazing at. Make this a sharing of love between you and God. Feel that God is sending you love from all around into your heart whenever you breathe in. When you breathe out, feel you are sending God love from your spiritual eye to wherever you are gazing. Feel God's presence all around and specifically at your gaze point. You can be looking around during this exercise or you can choose to gaze at one singular point, try it each way.

Adding a simple mantra can help you focus on the feeling of love energy being shared.

Mentally say "God" on the out breath as you are sending Him love. Other mantras could work like "Love" or "Aum." If you choose a complicated mantra, your attention may become too focused on the words and not feeling the love energy.

Most people when first starting meditation, will have trouble feeling energy in the heart and spiritual eye chakra. Here's a simple exercise to do for a few breaths when starting love breathing. It is only meant to use as an aid a few times when starting until you get the feel of it.

Right as you start to breath in, slap your right hand against the heart center and hold it there as you breathe in. Then immediately before you start to exhale, take your right hand and vigorously tap once your forehead with the fingers. Then as you exhale, let your right hand slowly move away from your forehead with palm facing up to indicate the love energy is going up to God.

Just do this about 5 times when starting. You can try tapping hard or soft, whatever helps you feel the love energy at these chakras. After doing this for a few days, you may not need to do it anymore.

Exercise 2a: Practice Love Breathing sitting right where you are for 5 minutes.

Exercise 2b: Practice Love Breathing several times throughout the day for at least a minute each time. Ideal times to practice love breathing are:

> *when riding in a car, bus, or train*
> *sitting in front of a computer*
> *sitting in your car*
> *waiting in line at a store*
> *sitting on a park bench*
> *attending a boring meeting*
> *taking a walk.*

Exercise 2c: Continue taking unstructured, daily loving God walks.

LOVE BREATH
Inhale

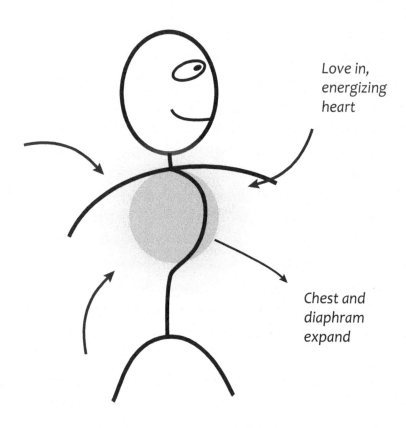

Love in,
energizing
heart

Chest and
diaphram
expand

Mind focuses on energizing heart,
with God's love

LOVE BREATH
Exhale

God!

Love out
to God

Chest and
diaphram
contract

Mind focuses on loving God

3. Basic Love Breathing Walking Meditation

The best location for a walking meditation is right outside where you live, so that you can easily go for one on a regular basis. Straight residential streets are excellent and an ideal place to start.

Walk for at least 30 minutes while doing love breathing. Keep your head level, but try to look up about 45 degrees if possible. Looking up is hard when first starting, so don't get overly concerned if you can't maintain this when beginning. Try to look up a little though and certainly don't look down except to make sure you don't trip. Keep your posture erect with your chest puffed out a little. This helps open up your heart chakra.

As best as possible stay in a straight line. You can walk back and forth along a stretch several hundred yards long. Ideally there would be long enough stretch to just go out and come back once for the full 30 minutes. Every turn does add a distraction. By staying on the same street, you will become "bored" with the scenery, this makes it easier to go inward and not just look at the sights.

After you are done with the walk, immediately go and sit, with eyes closed, in meditation. Use your normal meditation technique if you already meditate. If not, you can just do the love breathing with closed eyes. However, love breathing isn't the best technique to use for a closed-eye meditation. I would recommend the Hong-Sau meditation technique. It is easy to find online resources about it.

Many people who have tried this walking meditation comment that the sitting meditation at the end is the best part and that they have much deeper sitting meditations after the walk. The walk does bring up a lot of energy that should internalized afterwards, otherwise you could be left feeling unbalanced.

It is recommended you do this basic walking meditation for at least 5 times before going on.

Exercise 3:

Take a 30-minute Love Breathing Walking Meditation.

Then sit for at least 5-10 minutes in meditation after the walk.

Continue doing this every day or at least several days a week.

4. Coaxing

This walking meditation allows one to coax themselves into a state of still joy. When the art of self-coaxing is mastered, one can systematically go from being agitated to peaceful upliftment. It is a remarkable, repeatable process.

To describe self-coaxing, it's beneficial to use a simplistic model of spiritual evolution.

We can see ourselves as ego bubbles floating in the infinite consciousness of God's love and joy. For some unknown reason, we have constructed the walls of this ego bubble to make ourselves separate. This separation is the cause of all our pain and suffering. To mask the pain, we routinely distract our mind with random thoughts and fulfilling physical desires. Unfortunately, these activities increase our ego separation and lead to more pain.

To get back to God's infinite joy, we need to dissolve the ego by realizing our oneness with God. We do this by silencing "the monkey mind" and opening our hearts to God.

Now, in a state of agitation, where your mind is restless with random thoughts, one can through sheer willpower quiet the mind quickly by silencing all or almost all thoughts. The problem with this approach, though, is it leaves you inside your ego bubble, in a void, separate from God with no distractions. The utter nothingness is too painful to bear. Typically, as one starts to silence their minds, fear arises, the fear of being in this void, this nothingness. A classic flight/fight response to fear kicks in and your mind rebels against the silence and opens up a flood of random thoughts to escape the void.

This dynamic is what makes meditation so challenging and so difficult to tame "the monkey mind."

Exercise 4a: Experience pushing too hard.
On your next walk, right at the beginning, immediately silence all thoughts. Immediately start looking up at one fixed point in front of you. Do not look around at all, totally ignore all people, cars, bikes passing you by. Practice love breathing. Using tremendous willpower, try and keep this going for at least 10 minutes. Then relax, look around.

For most people, this exercise will bring up intense resistance, be difficult, painful, cause your breathing to increase due to fear and may be impossible to even do. If you experienced this, congratulations! You have found the borderline between your ego and God! This knowledge can help you in bringing down this border!

God's love and joy is needed to fill the voids left from quieting the mind. Loving God dissolves or pokes holes in the wall of our egos, letting His grace come shining in. This dispels the fear and allows us to further quiet the mind and open our hearts more, letting more of God's love in. This becomes a self-reinforcing process of opening more and more to God.

But in order to focus on loving God, you first need to stop the plethora of random thoughts without triggering an insurmountable egoic fight/flight response. You can keep the mind busy subconsciously by moving the body, walking, and looking around. Just walking and looking around can consume a large part of your mental capacity, making it easier to quiet random thoughts, so you can focus on loving God.

Here is a description of the Coaxing Process during a typical 30-minute walking meditation:

Start to 10 minutes   Calming Down

The monkey mind is in full distraction mode with random thoughts running wild.

If you try to immediately silence the mind, you will probably fail or make the walk so unpleasant you will not want to keep up a regular practice.

So instead. walk faster than normal, just look around at the sights, not up, but not down either. Practice love breathing. Feel God's love in everything you see. Feel like you are receiving God's love from everything you see and sending it back out to everything you are looking at.

By walking faster than normal and looking around, much of your mental processing capacity will be used up and thus unable to engage in random thoughts that would take you away from focusing on loving God.

10 minutes to 20 minutes   Striving for Communion

Here you might start to calm and start to feel God's peaceful presence.

Walk at a normal or slightly slower than normal pace. Start looking up, but allow yourself to look around some. Engage your willpower to start silencing thoughts. Focus more on love breathing.

20 minutes to 30 minutes   Striving for Union

Here a calm, peaceful joy may have emerged.

Start walking very slow. Looking up, keep your eyes fixed in place and keep your head fixed relative to your body. So, the only way to look in a different direction is when you turn your body when needed. Ignore any people walking by, bicyclists, or cars. Focus completely on quieting the mind and love breathing. Let time collapse, let go of any thoughts of past or future, love God in the eternal now.

Initially, this last stage, of keeping your eyes fixed, probably will be very difficult for most people. If so, just keep looking around instead and maybe try fixing your gaze for only a few seconds at a time.

A typical inclination, during a walking meditation, is to try too hard at the beginning and not hard enough at the end.

People want to "go deep" immediately at the beginning and may try to force "instant quiet" on the mind. I personally have never been able to do this; it always takes about 15 minutes to feel the "calm upliftment." I think one of biggest reasons people stop trying walking meditation (or any meditation) is they try too hard initially, causing the ego to rebel and they give up in discouragement. Much better to ease into it and then keep going.

Towards the end of a walk, one may have entered a pleasant calm, joyous state. The natural inclination is to relax and just enjoy it as is. But instead, one can make great strides by totally focusing on loving and feeling God everywhere, while actively letting go of all other thoughts. In a short amount of time at the end, you can find yourself going deeper than you ever expect, you just need 100% totally focused effort for the last 5 to 10 minutes.

The whole coaxing process is a continuous process. It is described here in 3 stages to make it easier to communicate. The key to making walking meditation enjoyable and meaningful every single time is to master this coaxing process. To be able to sense when you are pushing too hard and sense when you are not pushing enough. Depending on your mood on a particular day, how much and when you push yourself will vary. With enough practice, walking meditation becomes something to look forward to, something that brings up a feeling of anticipated joy, as you realize you will end up happier and calmer than when you started, and it won't require any unbearable exertion of will power.

Exercise 4b: Pace Experimentation:
Try walking at different paces. Throughout your walk quickly change from fast to slow, slow to fast. Feel the difference it makes in your ability to focus on loving God, your ability to quiet the mind. In particular feel how going very slow at the beginning makes it very challenging, whereas going very slow at the end allows you to much deeper than if you kept walking at a normal pace. Do this for as many times as it takes for you to get a good feel what an optimal pace is for you, given your agitation and calmness level.

Exercise 4c: Gaze Experimentation:
Experiment where you gaze and how much you shift your gaze. Try looking down for an entire walking meditation. How does it feel? In particular, make sure you try looking up about 45 degrees along a fixed line of sight for the last 5 minutes of a walk, keep your eyes completely motionless relative to your head. Your gaze point will only change as you walk forward or make a turn. Notice how this increases an energy flow upward into your head. It can feel like blood is rushing up, pressuring and expanding your brain. Do this for as many times as it takes to get a good feel for how to optimize your gaze from looking around at the beginning of a walk, to only looking up in a fixed line of sight. Optimize your "gaze quieting" to help you go deeper without bringing up debilitating ego resistance.

The following tables, diagrams, graphs, attempt to communicate this coaxing process visually. They reflect my background in business and engineering. Please feel free to disregard if such communication style doesn't communicate to you.

Coaxing progression over a 30 minute meditation walk

	Troubled	Calm	Joyful	Blissful
Heart	Troubled	Calm	Joyful	Blissful
Mind/ focus	let thoughts run wild, while feeling God's love through everything seen	try to let go of thoughts, while loving God at the gaze point		maximum effort to clear all thoughts, feel one with God in love
Pace	Faster than normal	Normal	Slower than normal	Very slow
Gaze	Looking around at scenery	Looking up and around	Looking up at one point, noticing people passing	Looking up at one point, ignoring everything else
Normal impulse	Push yourself too hard, trying to suppress all thoughts			Push yourself too little, happy w/ joy rather than fixing gaze and clearing all thoughts to get to bliss

Time in minutes: 0   5   10   15   20   25   30

Coaxing to stillness

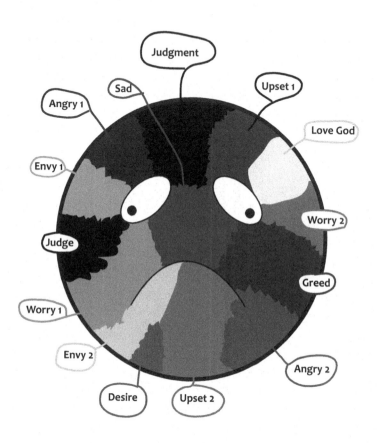

Good luck quieting this mind down instantaneously!

It's extremely difficult to force a restless mind to start loving God.

Coaxing to stillness

Rather than force your mind to stillness, keep it busy in an outward activity that occupies your mind but doesn't take too much conscious thought. This helps prevent it from going off on random thought trains.

Coaxing to stillness

As the heart and mind still, reduce the amount of outward activity. This frees extra mind capacity to focus more on loving God.

Coaxing to stillness

When still enough, ceasing outward activity
can help lead into a deep loving
communion/ meditation.

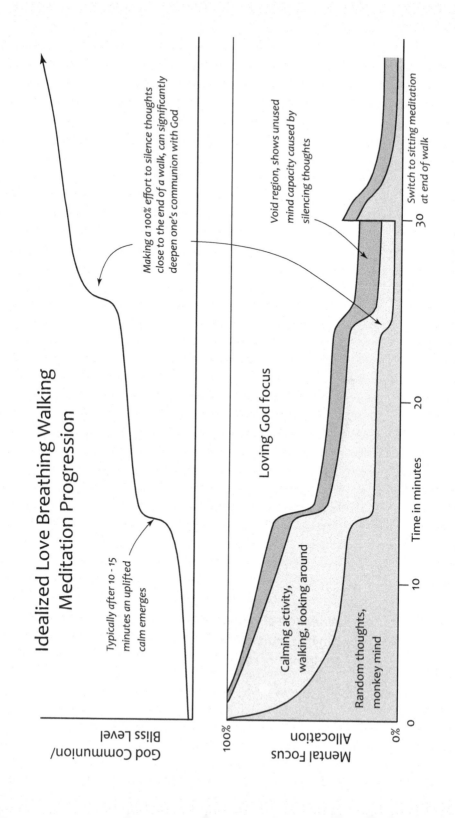

Idealized Love Breathing Walking Meditation Progression

Typically after 10 - 15 minutes an uplifted calm emerges

Making a 100% effort to silence thoughts close to the end of a walk, can significantly deepen one's communion with God

God Communion/Bliss Level

Void region, shows unused mind capacity caused by silencing thoughts

Loving God focus

Calming activity, walking, looking around

Random thoughts, monkey mind

Mental Focus Allocation

100%

0%

0   10   20   30

Time in minutes

Switch to sitting meditation at end of walk

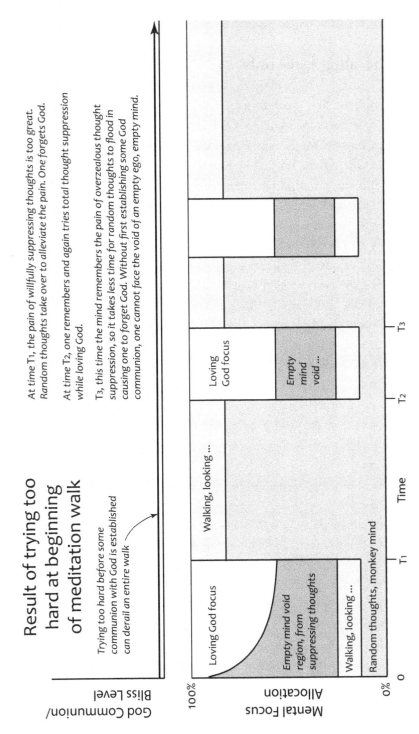

Result of trying too hard at beginning of meditation walk

Trying too hard before some communion with God is established can derail an entire walk

At time T1, the pain of willfully suppressing thoughts is too great. Random thoughts take over to alleviate the pain. One forgets God.

At time T2, one remembers and again tries total thought suppression while loving God.

T3, this time the mind remembers the pain of overzealous thought suppression, so it takes less time for random thoughts to flood in causing one to forget God. Without first establishing some God communion, one cannot face the void of an empty ego, empty mind.

God Communion/ Bliss Level

Mental Focus Allocation

100%

0%

0   T1   Time   T2   T3

Loving God focus

Empty mind void region, from suppressing thoughts

Walking, looking ...

Random thoughts, monkey mind

Walking, looking ...

Loving God focus

Empty mind void ...

5. Sending Love only

When I first started these walks, a strong intuition came to first only focus on sending God love, don't focus on receiving God's love. So, for 2 weeks that is what I did, then a feeling came it was OK to focus on sharing love with God.

This was an important step for me, since up to that time my spiritual search and practice was selfish, I was focused on feeling better for myself and overcoming unhappiness. Outwardly serving others had become part of my practice through my church, but inwardly it was all about feeling good inside my ego.

For the two weeks, I walked, and sent love to God on each out breath. While doing this I imagined God becoming happier with each breath of love I sent. I felt Him rejoicing with each breath received. I imagined him responding like the prodigal son's father receiving his wayward son joyously, with open arms. Since I breathe about 12 breaths a minute, I imagined God celebrating 12 times a minute my loving return to Him. The purpose of my walk was to make God happier, not myself happy. But of course, the more I inwardly focused on making God happier, the happier I became.

Exercise 5:

Start your meditation walk with the intent 'my only purpose for this walk is to make God happier.' Feel for the next 30 minutes the only purpose in life is to make God happier. Then, imagine God rejoicing with each love-breath you send Him. Feel God up in sky, at your gaze point, smiling at you, celebrating joyously each time you finish breathing out and sending Him a ray of love.

Do this for a least for 1-2 weeks. After you can go back to sharing love with God, rather than just sending it.

God yearns for our love ... what is God longing for? Our love. Our attention. He has made it very difficult for Himself, because He gave man free will to seek Him or reject Him. He says, "I am pursuing every heart, waiting for My children to spurn My creation and turn toward Me." ... unless we choose to go to Him willingly, He cannot free us or Himself from suffering.

—Paramhansa Yogananda

Any parent grieves when their children ignore or turn away from them. God, as the divine parent of us all, also grieves this way and like any parent is overjoyed when we, His children, turn back, call home, or send our love.

6. Self-condemnation

This can be a major obstacle to spiritual unfoldment. Feeling upset at yourself for any reason, limits our perception to being small and separate from God, not a happy place. God only wants our love and He loves us unconditionally despite our faulty actions or thoughts.

Repetitive ongoing failure will be a constant companion during a love breathing walking meditation. It will be impossible to focus on loving God on every single every breath. When I started out, even focusing for only 1 in about 5 breaths was a victory and still is! Learning to deal constructively with this ongoing, breath-to-breath failure is one of the great spiritual opportunities a love breathing walking meditation has to offer. Be grateful for the opportunity this affords, rather than upset for the difficulties.

If you forget to love God with every breath while walking, you could get angry at yourself and whip yourself mentally to get yourself back to focusing on God. However, this is quite painful and it sets up a subconscious learning that associates remembering God with pain. After a while your mind, wanting to avoid pain, learns to not remember God after you have forgotten Him. If through sheer willpower, you keep a walking meditation practice going while punishing yourself every time you forget God, over time you will remember Him less and less, until finally you give up the practice altogether.

Instead, make remembering God a joyful experience, so you will remember more and more!

God is overjoyed every time we remember Him, and especially every time we send Him some love. Like the father in the prodigal son parable, God celebrates when we inwardly turn back towards Him. We should join in on this celebration!

Exercise 6: Dedicate your entire walking meditation to celebrating with God every time you remember Him. Let this be your sole focus for at least a week.

When walking you undoubtably will start thinking about something random and forget to keep sharing love with God with every breath. Once you remember and send God some love on your out-breath, feel God up at your gaze point, smiling and celebrating your "return." Sense Him thanking you for this little breath of love. Even if this feels like pretend or just your imagination, keep doing it. Over time it will open the doorways of your heart to God.

Over a normal 30-minute walk, you may have dozens of opportunities to celebrate your "return" to God! So instead of being upset with forgetting God, now it becomes a joyous celebration every time you remember and send Him another love-breath.

Practicing this *"Joyful Remembrance"* while walking provides a wonderful means to habitualize accepting God's unconditional love for us. During a walk, it is relatively easy to imagine God's gratitude and love to us for just the smallest amounts of love we send him on each breath. It is always better to practice anything when it is easy and then move on to more difficult situations.

Additional exercise: Whenever you feel upset with yourself for any reason, stand up, start love breathing and feel God loving you unconditionally right now, in the Eternal Now, despite whatever wrong action or thought you have done. This takes great spiritual courage, is difficult, and affords great spiritual benefit.

7. Too Despondent

During a difficult time in life, you may feel so despondent that you can't even send God love, feel gratitude, or even consider feeling peaceful or joyful. If taking a walking meditation while despondent, it is usually better not to try and force yourself to send love to God or force yourself to feel gratitude. Instead just love God with longing, longing for His comfort. Breathe in God's loving comfort from all around into your heart as normal, but when breathing out, feel yourself sending God, out from your spiritual eye, a longing plea to be saved by Him. Many of my own walks, when I first started this practice, were just walks longing for God on each breath. Indeed, you make it an exercise in trying to long for God more and more, deeper and deeper with each breath.

You may find partway into the walk; you start feeling uplifted. At that point, it would be more helpful to start practicing love breathing as normal by sending God love on the out breath.

If you keep only longing after feeling uplifted, you will prevent yourself from going deeper into communion with God.

Exercise 7a: Start your walking meditation longing for God as described above. If you aren't feeling despondent, lonely, or depressed, just do this for a minute or two to get a feel for it. Then resume sharing love normally. If you are despondent, do it for as long as needed.

Exercise 7b: If you are feeling so despondent that even a walk is too much, try sitting alone on a comfortable couch or chair with your eyes open. Slouch, don't try sitting upright, then practice love breathing with longing for God while looking around or just staring off into space, whichever is easier. Feel God's comforting love come in to the heart while breathing in, then send a longing plea for more of God's comfort through the spiritual eye on the out-breath. Do this for as long as needed. After a few minutes you may feel slightly uplifted. Then it may be better to start sitting upright and go into a meditation with eyes closed.

I used this "slouched sitting" many, many times early on. If I was in a depressed state and I tried to meditate sitting upright, invariably I failed no matter how long I tried. Yet when I just sat and did "slouching love breathing with longing, staring off into space," I could in a few minutes, go from despondency to uplifted and start a regular meditation. It is another form of coaxing oneself rather than trying to force oneself.

8. Flavors of Love

What is your favorite flavor of God's love?

Mine is delight.

The love you share with God can carry different facets, different feelings, different "flavors." For instance, you may feel a great gratitude while loving God, or longing, or joy, or devotion, or ... The list is endless.

The main ones I've focused on are comfort, gratitude, delight, joyful, ecstatic. The previous section describes comfort, breathing in God's loving comfort with each breath, when you are feeling down, despondent and not able to tap into God's joy.

You can try sharing love with gratitude on a walk. When you send God love on the out-breath, do it with a sense of gratitude, gratitude for anything God has given you, but most especially gratitude for God's love. Then on the in-breath, feel God sending you love and God being grateful to you! Parents are usually grateful for their children; God is always grateful for His children. It is good to affirm God's loving gratitude for us. This takes great courage; imagining God is grateful for us. But it is true and the more we can accept it, the more we move closer to God.

The same with delight. You can send God love while delighting in Him. Likewise when you breath in God's love, feel Him delighting in you. Feel God being happy just because you exist, no other reason! And do it on every in-breath.

I view these flavors on a spectrum. If feeling low, comfort is the flavor to focus on. Then as I feel more uplifted, I can go through the other ones, ultimately ending up in joyful ecstasy (every now and then). You need to pick the best flavor for where you are currently. For instance, if I am feeling down or frustrated and then try to share joyful love with God, it doesn't work. Instead I need to "backtrack" to receiving comforting love. Then after awhile, usually in the same walk, but not always, I can shift into sharing love with gratitude or delight.

Delight is my favorite, because it affirms a close intimate happy relationship with God. It affirms God is my upbeat, spiritual friend. Usually after loving God with delight for a few minutes, it will shift into a joyous love sharing, not necessarily joy because of each other, just loving joy for all.

Exercise 8: Develop your own list of flavors of God's love. It can include the ones above and/or any other names meaningful to you. Then on your walks try them out. Note how it feels, how it feels differently when you focus on a different love flavor. See if you can find out which flavor is best for the range of moods you experience. See if you can experience a natural progression during the same walk of moving through flavors. Tune into when it is right for you to shift "up" and when shifting "up" is premature.

---

9. Lack of progress frustration

If you have a regular walking meditation practice, undoubtably, some walks will be uplifted, even ecstatic, while other walks won't be. The same is true with any spiritual practice. We all have had spiritual expansive experiences, times when we felt more joy, more love, more consciousness than we normally do. Most, actually almost all, of the time we are in a state less conscious, less joyful than some previous state. This can lead to frustration, since we carry the memory of being more, both consciously and unconsciously.

The memory of a better time can be a powerful ally on the spiritual path. However, the frustration the memory brings can become a serious hazard that trips us off the path.

Remembering a better time brings up a desire or yearning to feel it again.

If your desire, focuses only on pulling this joy into the confines of your own limited ego, separate from God, failure results and frustration arises. This frustration can turn to anger. Indeed, the anger can become so great it clouds your judgement. Remembering peak spiritual experiences then becomes associated with pain and anger! The mind lacking clarity, goes into defense mode and lets the fog of forgetfulness enter to alleviate the pain.

Luckily this desire, this yearning to return to spiritual expansiveness can be a catalyst for opening up more to God, for letting Him in to help melt the borders of your ego away. Appreciation and patience can turn this yearning towards expansion rather than frustration. When you start to yearn, when you start to feel a little frustration, quickly thank God for the previous love, the previous expansiveness you have experienced. Start loving God with gratitude for any love, any joy you have received. Also, then cultivate an inner faith that these times will return, and that those expanded states are your true home.

Think how much happier the prodigal son would have been on his journeys if he prayed with gratitude that he would eventually return home, knowing he would go back there someday into the safety and care of his father's house.

Exercise 9: Dedicate walks to loving God with gratitude for past spiritual experiences

For a week, at the beginning of your meditation walk, think about a peak spiritual experience you have had. Then love God with gratitude for this experience, thank God for giving you this preview of what will become your common experience. Then cultivate a calm, inner faith that this is where you are going. Thank God in advance for your eventual return home!

Additional Exercise:

Whenever you feel frustrated in life, breathe deeply, do a few love breaths to God and thank him that your current predicament is only temporary. Love Him in the eternal now.

---

10. Lack of willpower to try

What do you do when you are too unmotivated to try? When the thought of putting out even a little bit of focused effort is too much?

Well, you could do what most people do and wait until your suffering in life becomes so great, that you start making spiritual efforts in earnest.

The perceived spiritual benefit must be higher than the perceived spiritual effort needed, for anyone to muster the willpower to try and make an effort.

Unfortunately, usually the perceived benefit grows in time, not because we see a higher and higher potential for joy, but because our lives sink or tragedy hits. Then the benefit seems huge; just going from our low state to getting back to a remembered, previous, happy state.

One way to keep the "willpower to try" alive is to remember your higher states of joy. Keep the memory of them alive, with gratitude to God for them. Keep your "perceived benefit" huge.

The other way to encourage your spiritual efforts, is to make the "perceived effort" small, really small. So very small that virtually no willpower is needed to start.

The beauty of taking a spiritual walk is that it takes virtually no will power to start. You simply start walking. Then as you walk you apply just a little bit of willpower to focus on God. Only apply as much willpower as comfortable, with absolutely no strain. As you walk more and more, gradually, gently, God will come in more and more and help you. You may find at the end of the walk you are totally engaged with God and putting your entire effort into it.

Exercise 10: When feeling unmotivated, go for a walk. Tell yourself 'this will just be a normal walk, I'll let my mind and gaze wonder randomly, unchecked. I will just relax and not try to commune with God.' Then as you walk, if and only if, you start to feel a little calm, gently start a little love breathing. If it feels comfortable, start focusing more and more on it. But don't, if you don't feel like it. Do this any day you feel very unmotivated.

I've found this "just go for a walk, not a walking meditation" gets me outside on difficult days when the resistance to making any effort is high. But once walking, inevitably I end up doing a walking meditation and by the end of the walk putting a 100% effort into communing with God. After the walk, I'm always thankful I took it.

I am still amazed that my ego continues to get tricked every time I do this.

11. Praying for others

Seeing and feeling God in others becomes a wonderful way to pray for them. Part of a walk can be dedicated for this and even when not walking, love breathing can be used to pray this way. Try this right now while you are sitting down with your eyes open.

First practice simple love breathing for a moment. Just breathe in deeply, energize the heart center, silently chant "God" on the out-breath, while feeling love for Him. Then, pick someone you can see or if you are alone picture someone you know. While looking at the person, keep energizing your own heart on the in-breath, but on the out-breath, feel God loving this other person. Sense God's ecstatic love for this person's soul and His sheer delight in their being.

After a moment of this, shift your perception to seeing God *as* this other person. Feel that God is manifesting Himself as this person and relishing the experience of unfolding Himself in the life of this person. Feel God is the actor playing the part of this person and thoroughly enjoying Himself being in this play.

This is a progressive method of praying that I find helps me feel more love for the person, than if I just immediately mentally said a prayer for them.

The technique is simple:

First, get into a calm connection yourself with God, by love breathing.

Second, see God loving them with every breath.

Third, see God being them with every breath.

Seeing God love the person rather than you just sending them love directly, can be very helpful especially if you are praying for someone you have difficulties with. Even when you are praying for people you know and love, sometimes some of your ego feelings can get in the way. But if you are just focusing on God loving them, it becomes easier to feel divine love surrounding them.

Seeing God as someone is a key to loving unconditionally, both others and yourself. When we can see God just playing a role as another person, even a person who has acted badly or wronged you, we can start to see all the drama this person has caused as just a play, a play God puts on for His entertainment. But the Soul of everyone remains a part of God and ultimately each Soul will exit this worldly play. After the final curtain call, we all will attend the same casting party and meet the One Director.

Exercise 11a:

In the middle of a meditation walk, dedicate a few minutes to seeing God in someone. Picture them up at your gaze point surrounded and loved by God. Then feel God being them and thoroughly enjoying the role. Do this with people you love and also do this with some people you have difficulties with.

I find the middle of a walk is the best time to pray for others this way. In the middle of a walk, I've calmed down, started to feel a connection with God and can focus on God loving them. However, towards the end of a walk, if I focus on praying for others, it can prevent me from going into a deeper communion with God. At this point, the overwhelming desire is to just experience God alone, nothing else. So usually I'll pray for others in the middle of a walk, not at the end.

Exercise 11b:
When you see someone passing by while walking, feel God loving them for a breath or a few breaths. Or see God enjoying being them for a breath or few. Do this for the first half of your walk, then just focus on God alone.

Exercise 11c:
Next time you are standing in line, waiting, pick someone you can see and pray for them this way. See God loving them, then see God delighting in being them. Do this for the rest of your life!

Praying for others this way is also a wonderful way to get outside yourself, to help you stop thinking so much about yourself. It helps make your spiritual practice less self-centered, (self with a little "s" or ego-self).

Exercise 11d:
Feel God as playing the part of you, enjoying living your life with all its ups and downs. Realize He has been the one acting out all bad and good scenes from your life. He sees it all as a play and loves unconditionally the role of you, despite how He cast you.

12. Intuition and Creativity

Walking meditations enhance your intuition and creativity. By helping silence distracting thoughts, opening up your heart and mind to God, true intuition and creativity can flow in. This will happen naturally as you practice. Many times, I find on a walk, ideas flowing in about what to do next concerning different aspects of my life. Thoughts about issues I was not even thinking about. Indeed, it becomes almost as if your life is being directed and you just have to listen and then act. Also there comes a calmness about events even when you don't see a clear path ahead, because you know it will happen and a path will be revealed in time. Trusting in God becomes more of a reality, the more we love Him.

If you have a certain issue you want guidance or inspiration on, you can dedicate a walking meditation to it. After you are deeply into a walk, probably halfway through or more, ask God your question. Then listen for His answer. The listening part can take great willpower. We all want naturally to solve our problems and think about them endlessly. Asking God for an answer and then shutting off the thinking mind to just listen doesn't seem to come naturally.

It seems best to ask for guidance in the middle of a walk for the same reasons is seems best to pray for others in the middle of a walk. In the middle, usually a nice communion is established through which some true intuition can flow. Yet at the end of a walk, you may not want to be thinking about your projects and just want God alone. If you try to listen for some project specific intuition at the end, it may prevent you from going deeper into God.

Exercise 12: On your next walk, think about an issue, any issue you want some guidance on. It can be anything, business related, family issues, technical design challenges, writings ... Think about the issue after you have warmed up in your walk, probably about one third to halfway through. Ask God for guidance on the issue, don't make the question too specific, leave room for God to give you the answer you need, not want. Then for at least 5 minutes afterwards, silence your mind and just listen with 100% of your focus.

When I've done this, the first minute or two of listening takes tremendous willpower. But after listening in mental silence for a few minutes, many times an unexpected inspiration will come. Make sure though to ground any intuition as Paramahansa Yogananda described 'in common sense.'

13. Love God as the Eternal Now

Virtually all egoic thoughts are time and separation dependent. When we focus on loving God in just this instantaneous moment, thoughts and egoic identity simply fade away. It's a wonderful remarkable, and freeing process. Rather than struggling to overcome the ego, or struggling to suppress the monkey mind, one just needs to love God in the instantaneous moment, putting all thoughts of past or future on hold.

When walking, one can focus on feeling unity with all nature, all space, around them. This can be a very useful practice, indeed one I focused on exclusively for a time.

When I started, though, to focus on "being in the moment" when walking, it became easier, and simpler, to catch little sparks of God's ecstasy. Note that easier doesn't mean easy. I just find it more efficient to focus on loving God in the instantaneous moment than focusing on feeling unity with everything. This applied when walking, but not when sitting in a closed-eye meditation. When sitting in a closed-eye meditation, for me, it seems more efficient to focus on feeling your consciousness filling all space.

One possible explanation for this difference is that when looking at objects and focusing on feeling unity, it can become an exercise where you try to merge and project your ego out, rather than let it go. Also, it seems to be easier to directly suspend a sense of time, than directly suspend a sense of separation when your eyes are open, looking at distinct objects.

Exercise 13a:

Where you are sitting or standing now, start love breathing and looking at some fixed point. Let all sense of time, past, future dissolve. Do this for a few minutes.

Exercise 13b:

Notice how stillness overcomes your body in direct relation to how much you can just focus on the moment. Likewise, when you still your body it becomes easier to love God in the moment. So, while sitting and looking out and up at a fixed point, still your entire body, feel like every atom in it is going still. Then start love breathing and loving God in this instant.

Exercise 13c:

During the last 5-10 minutes of a walking meditation, on the out breath, feel like God and you are loving each other throughout infinity. Feel like you are merging with everything and everything you can see.

Do this for a few walks.

Exercise 13d:

During the last 5-10 minutes of a walking meditation, gazing up at a fixed point, feel like you are loving God in this moment. Let feelings of past and future go, only now. Do this for a few walks. See if there is any difference for you doing it this way compared to the previous exercise.

14. Devotional Stepping Stone

Love Breathing continues to offer me a way to experience, from time to time, love & joy beyond definitions, beyond even the thought of God & I. Sometimes on a walk, toward the end of it, even chanting "God" on the out-breath becomes a distraction, a distraction away from feeling love & joy everywhere.

Wanting to, trying to rush myself into this state, remains one of my biggest challenges on a walk. Many times, in the middle of a walk, during the warm-up state, I'll try to just imagine myself experiencing love everywhere, joy everywhere, without chanting "God," with forcing my mind silent. Usually, always, it doesn't work. When I catch myself trying too hard, too fast, I simply go back to sharing love with God, to feeling God & I delighting in each other. Invariably focusing on this "devotional stepping stone state" results in a much deeper and more joyous communion with the divine.

The power, and probably necessity for most, of spiritual devotion is under appreciated by many spiritual seekers today. Yet devotion is a key stepping stone for spiritual progress. Without it, spiritual practice usually becomes a dry, mental affair that fails to inspire one enough to continue.

Exercise 14: For an entire walk, don't share love with God. Instead feel like you are loving the world yourself. Energize your heart on the in-breath, then on the out-breath feel as though it is you sending your love out into the world through the spiritual eye.

Where does this take you? Compare it to practicing devotional sharing with God first and then only at the very end of your walk, try feeling love & joy everywhere beyond even the word God.

This is a way to compare and experience the wondrous effectiveness of devotion as a spiritual practice.

Expanded Discussions

Several topics are discussed in more depth here.

The Sweet Spot

As mentioned, mastering the coaxing process requires sensing when you are pushing too hard and when not pushing enough. It requires finding the sweet spot where just the right amount of effort maximizes your focus on loving God, without pushing your ego into successful rebellion.

This sweet spot is determined by your state of restlessness, your state of disconnection from God. The more restless you are the less you can silence random thoughts without triggering an ego revolt. The figure on page 83 outlines this state. With practice you can quickly find this sweet spot of effort quickly and stay in it throughout an entire walk.

As you become more still, as your connection with God grows, the amount of effort you can apply to loving God increases, see page 84. Naturally as your mind stills, you are able to focus on loving God more. Also though, and interestingly so, the more you have opened up to God, the more your "communion/bliss level" has increased, the more you can withstand the pain of silencing random thoughts.

On page 58, notice in the figure how at the beginning of a walk, when there is little God communion, no effort is put into silencing thoughts, i.e. no "void region." Then as God communion grows one can put more effort into silencing thoughts, the void region can increase. With more of God's bliss flowing in, one can better tolerate the pain of a silent ego. Notice how towards the end of a 30 minute walk the void region increases as one totally focuses on loving God.

This last 5 to 10 minutes of a meditation walk are exquisitely blissful while also excruciatingly painful. The pain of immediately silencing all thoughts while trying 100% to let your ego dissolve. This pain coincides with a wonderful joy of God communion.

For me this experience relates, albeit on a much smaller scale, to an experience of Saint Teresa of Avila. In her autobiography, she writes about an angel piercing her heart with a spear:

> *"In his hands, I saw a golden spear, with an iron tip at the end that appeared to be on fire. He plunged it into my heart several times, all the way to my entrails. When he drew it out, he seemed to draw them out, as well, leaving me all on fire with love for God.*
>
> *The pain was so strong that it made me moan several times, and yet the sweetness of the pain was so surpassing that I couldn't possibly wish to be rid of it. My soul couldn't be content with anything but God. It wasn't a physical pain, but a spiritual one, … pain which gave me a greater bliss than any created things could give me."*

For me, it is wonderfully reassuring that through a simple meditation walk, anyone can experience, on a level they are ready for and willing to embrace, having some of their ego "entrails" drawn out to make room for the fire of God's love.

It is [my] business to look into the very face of God until [I] ache with bliss.

—Frank Laubach

For a given state of restlessness, there is an optimal outward activity level that helps one practice loving God

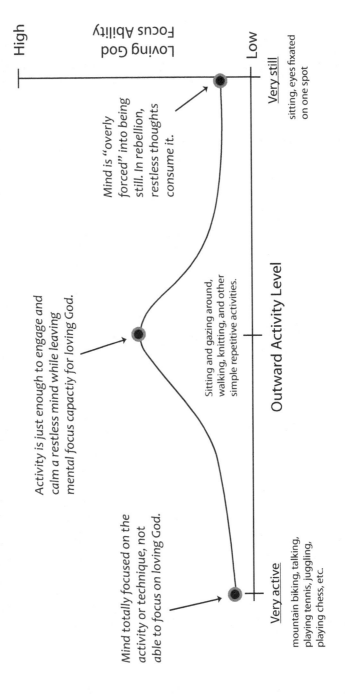

Loving God Focus Ability

High

Low

Mind totally focused on the activity or technique, not able to focus on loving God.

Activity is just enough to engage and calm a restless mind while leaving mental focus capactiy for loving God.

Mind is "overly forced" into being still. In rebellion, restless thoughts consume it.

Outward Activity Level

<u>Very active</u>
mountain biking, talking, playing tennis, juggling, playing chess, etc.

Sitting and gazing around, walking, knitting, and other simple repetitive activities.

<u>Very still</u>
sitting, eyes fixated on one spot

As the mind stills, the optimal activity level also stills

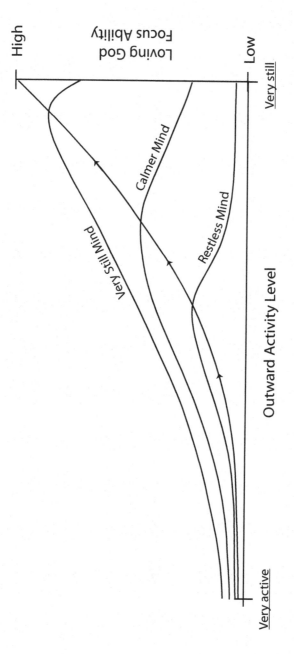

With sincere, unconditional practice, going from restless activity to joyful stillness can take just a few minutes.

Breathing

How should you breathe during a meditation walk: normal? slow? fast? deep? diaphragmatic?

In general I've found just breathing at a normal rate, but a little deeper than normal with each breath is best.

When I've tried to do slow, deep diaphragmatic breathing or some deep pranayam breathing techniques while walking it actually distracted away from devotional communion. Focusing on deep diaphragmatic or pranayam breathing while walking, took too much mental focus. I wasn't able to focus on loving God as much. Another issue; slow, deep breathing while walking left me short of breath and all my attention would shift into wanting more air.

You should experiment with your own breathing during walks. Do whatever helps you go deeper into a devotional communion. If the breathing technique starts to distract from communion, change it into something that aids, not hinders.

Interesting the last 5-10 minutes of my walks can be intense. Intense joy, even blissful communion, paired with an intense fear response at the same time. My heart rate can quicken even more at the end of a walk due to the fear response. Here I've found it is best to actually breath faster and deeper. Breathing faster helps deal with, helps mitigate the fear response. Breathing deeper helps enhance the communion.

All this to me is very counterintuitive. During normal sitting meditations, no intense fear response is triggered. My heart and breath slow right up until the end. I don't have a conceptual framework for understanding this aspect of "spiritual physiology." Luckily, conceptual understanding isn't necessary. Personal "trial and refinement" is enough. Try many things and see what works, let God guide you, which He will if given the chance.

Visual processing

Visual stimulus is a potent tool when coaxing the mind to stillness, when trying to calm oneself in general. Up to 2/3rds of the brain can be involved with processing visual sights. If one is in a state of restlessness with many random thoughts darting about, just looking around, especially at something moving, can provide a calming effect. Much of your brain will become involved with the visual processing, so less of it will be available to think random thoughts.

This is a major reason why watching ocean waves or a fire burning can be so soothing and entrancing. It also helps explain why when first sitting and closing eyes to meditate, one can initially feel less calm and experience more random thoughts. Just shutting your eyes, frees up a lot of brain capacity and cuts off a visual sense of ego identification. The ego gets scared and immediately uses the extra brain capacity for random thoughts to distract from the fear.

Intelligent and conscious use of "visual calming" can be an important ally in one's meditative practice. This is why at the start of a meditative walk, one looks around a lot, as much as one needs, to quell the random thought trains. Then by the end of the walk, one looks at a single point in the sky.

A good exercise to help appreciate visual calming is to sit and meditate on a beach. Try 3 different routines:

1. *Sit and immediately shut eyes to meditate.*
   One may experience a lot of ego resistance that will require substantial willpower to overcome in order to go into a deep meditation.

2. *Sit look at the waves until one is very still, then shut eyes to meditate. Comparatively, it probably will be easier to go into a deep mediation this way.*

3. *Sit and look at the waves with open eyes during the entire time, even while meditating. This way, one may remain calm, but continuing the visual stimulus throughout the entire mediation will distract one from going as deep.*

As a note, breathing routines and chanting are also very effective "calming tools" used in many meditative traditions to help coax one into deeper states without triggering an ego rebellion.

Focusing on the breath helps in part to ease one into a deeper meditative state by simply giving the mind something to do rather than thinking random thoughts. Once one is sufficiently calm and still, focus on the breath can then stop.

Likewise, devotional chanting before meditating takes the mind off random thoughts and opens the heart to God. This helps smooth the transition in a deeper meditative state without triggering fear-based ego resistance.

Eye position

Inwardly looking up with eyes closed, is a technique used in some spiritual meditative traditions, including the one I practice. It has been quite useful; it raises the energy flow and raises one's spirits. Indeed, if you watch people walking on the street, in general people looking up are happier, whereas people looking down are sadder.

When I first started taking walking meditations, I reasoned I should look up. Yet it took me a year to seriously try looking up. There was such a strong ego resistance to doing it. Finally, after a year I told myself, *"this is silly, you need to see if this will make the meditation walks better, try it … OK, I will force myself to try it for one week, I have enough willpower to handle that, but no longer."* Well after a few days, I experienced how much better and deeper the walks were when looking up. Now looking up is part of every walk.

At first, I tried looking up the entire walk, from beginning to end. This proved too stressful, as looking up caused a strong ego rebellion at the beginning of the walk, I found it unsustainable and too unenjoyable. Instead, now, it has become a strong tool in the coaxing process. I just look out and around when starting and then slowly over the entire walk transition to only looking at one point up in the sky at the end of the walk.

Walking location, direction, time

Where should one walk, how long, what pace, what direction? Answering these questions provides a fascinating exploration to embark on. One should try different locations to walk, different times, different directions, walk straight, walk in circles, walk a labyrinth, ... See how your ability to go deep is affected with different changes.

For myself, it became a fun, enthralling exploration to find the best walking "ways" to deepen my walking meditations. I can relate what I experience, which may or may not directly relate to what is best for others.

Walking straight on quiet residential streets has proved best for me. Actually, the best place I've found is a parking lot road in the back of a spiritual community close to my home. It's about 500 feet long and I go back and forth about 4 times (and then go meditate in their meditation temple).

Interestingly and unexpectantly, I found walking on forest trails out in nature not as effective. I love nature, in retirement I volunteer at a farm just to be outdoors and work in nature. But whenever I take a meditation walk in nature, my attention is drawn to nature, I cannot will myself to just love God directly. Instead, I must focus on loving God through nature. Also rather than looking up at a fixed point, I must look around, still with an upward gaze, feeling God in nature's beauty. The meditation walks in nature usually are more enjoyable and it's easier to enter into a calm communion. But a meditation walk, for me, on suburban streets usually ends up being deeper, more intensely blissful: very counterintuitive to me.

Taking love breathing walks on busy city streets works quite well also, it just takes practice. Like in nature, when in a city, I will look up but not at a fixed point.

Walking a straight line seems best, as whenever I take a turn, my attention is slightly distracted and it takes several steps to get back into the same focused communion level as before the turn. Ideally the walk would just be one straight line out 15 minutes, turn around and come back.

Avoiding the sun in your eyes is important when looking up. So, I prefer to walk north-south if possible, especially if early in the morning or later a night when the sun is low. Also, wearing visor cap helps to shade your eyes.

The ideal length of a walk seems to be 30 to 45 minutes. Any shorter and I cannot go as deep. Any longer and I find myself plateauing and cannot go deeper, so at that point it's just better to sit and meditate, where I can go deeper. Sitting to meditate after a walking meditation becomes just another step in the coaxing process into deeper stillness.

The pace of a walk helps with the coaxing process. Faster at first, then normal, then slow, then very slow. Walking very slow at the end 5 to 10 minutes really propels one deeper. At the end of a walk before going inside to meditate sitting, I will usually stand still outside while love breathing for a few minutes. Just another step to coax oneself into stillness.

Diving Deep during Sunday Service

This section relates how I use coaxing and love breathing to enhance my experience of Sunday service. While this isn't a walking meditation, it uses the same principles and provides a look at how coaxing can be used in other spiritual situations.

Sunday church service is a special time. In the company of many sincere souls, one's inner efforts to commune with God can be magnified many-fold compared to efforts done alone in private. Because of this wonderous "leverage," I focus on maximizing inspiration, God communion while attending Sunday service.

On the surface, the most straightforward way to get the most out of church seemed to simply get to church, run in quickly, sit down, close eyes and try to meditate as deeply as possible during the entire church service, while listening to the talks and music. This is the method I employed for over a decade. However, after experiencing the powerful uplifting effect of love breathing and coaxing while walking, I decided to see how these could be applied to Sunday service. The first step was to pray and ask God for inner guidance on how to make the most of Sunday service. Then to try out anything that comes to mind while observing the effect.

A multi-step procedure evolved, which I'm sure many will regard as overly refined and overly complex. But it works for me and may be useful to others.

First, I drive to church about 15 to 20 minutes early and park on a fairly busy street with cars constantly passing by. Then I sit in the car, practice love breathing while just looking all around for several minutes. As calmness descends, I look around less and less, until I am just looking straight ahead at the cars driving by. I continue love breathing while focusing on stilling my entire body. As I become stiller, I then look up at a fixed spot in the sky above the road. After a few more minutes of being completely still, with devotional fixation, I close my eyes and meditate for a few minutes, before getting out of the car and entering church.

Interesting, I had tried parking on a quiet side street for this initial "pre-church inner preparation phase." But looking out at an empty, still street proved too challenging, my mind needed more coaxing. Looking at moving cars is similar to looking at ocean waves or a fire in its calming effect and has proved a very useful coaxing step into stillness.

Once inside church, rather than try to meditate immediately, I will practice love breathing while looking around. I'll look at the pictures of Christ and of some Indian Masters which adorn the altar at my church while listening to the devotional chanting. As stillness descends again, I'll look around less and less, then look at one picture of Master, then I'll just look at a fixed blank space on the wall above the pictures of the Masters. Interestingly it is more effective for me to look at the blank wall when in a very still state rather than the picture of Master. When in a very still devotional state, I want to feel God everywhere around me and inside of me. If I am looking at a picture of Master, my focus becomes God as Master, in the picture. So, it becomes harder to feel God everywhere.

Shambhavi Mudra is an Indian spiritual technique of gazing upwards. Practicing love breathing at the same time adds a devotional focus to it.

When in this "devotional Shambhavi Mudra" state, the desire to shut my eyes and just meditate becomes intense, almost overwhelming. But I will resist the urge to quickly shut my eyes and hold this open, upward gaze position for several minutes. It feels very much like the last 5 minutes of a meditation walk. Very intense, complete focus on squelching all random thoughts, while going as still as possible into a devotional communion with God. Only after holding this state for at least 5 minutes and when the

Coaxing deep during Sunday service

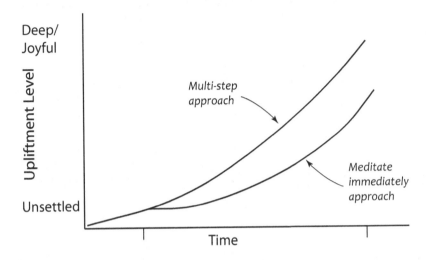

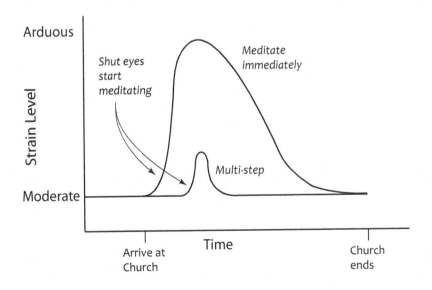

A multi-step coaxing approach is less stressful, yet can take one deeper and higher than a simple meditate right away approach.

urge to shut my eyes becomes overwhelming, then I'll shut my eyes and meditate for the rest of the service.

Counterintuitively, this multi-step approach has proved much more effective. My original thought was by shutting my eyes right away would leave me more time to meditate and thus go deeper. However, after many "comparison trials," the multi-step coaxing approach has always brought me to a deeper more uplifted state by the end of church service than if I simply only meditated immediately.

Sitting versus walking meditation observations

These are some random observations I've made when comparing sitting versus walking meditation.

Walking meditations are more energetic, can feel energy flows more throughout my body when walking. Sitting meditations are calmer, less awareness of the body.

I can go deeper in sitting meditations, can enter into deeper stillness, can feel greater sense of peace. In walking meditations I am more able to feel "sparkling joy."

The ending 5 to 10 minutes of walking meditation many times are excruciatingly joyful, a "heart piercing" as mentioned earlier. Some sitting meditations have been deeply blissful, but not excruciatingly so. I believe this difference arises since during a walking meditation you are simultaneously aware of the physical/ego level and the uplifted spiritual. Whereas in a sitting meditation, you can enter into just the uplifted spiritual level without suffering having to hold on to physical/ego awareness at the same time.

I can more consistently and reliably enter into an uplifted state with a walking meditation. Walking stimulates the spines energy, then channeling it up makes it easier to feel uplifted.

During a walking meditation, the challenge is to not be distracted by worldly sites and worldly thoughts. In sitting meditation, the larger challenge is to keep from going into subconsciousness or a sleep state.

The seasons

During winter from about Christmas to the end of March, my walking meditations become much deeper, more intensely joyful. Then every spring I am surprised when the depth of them lessens. Remorse sets in and always I vow; next winter I will make an extra effort to go deep during winter, the seemingly easiest season to do so for me. I am not sure why this is. It may be simply that I prefer cooler weather and the normally cloudy weather in winter adds a "cloistered" feel to the air. Other people have mentioned, they prefer taking walks under a bright blue sky.

Loving God with every breath, every step

Perhaps the greatest benefit of practicing love breathing walking meditation is that it creates a habit of loving God with every breath, every step. Over time, it becomes an automatic habit, one simply starts whenever walking or even whenever breathing!

Many times, during a normal day I'll find myself automatically love breathing, feeling God, in my heart, in my mind. This happens routinely when doing mundane chores, walking somewhere, standing in line, sitting quietly, … It's like sipping from a wellspring of joy bubbling up throughout the day. Transitory trials remain, but only as perturbations against an unchanging background tapestry of God.

Time for a walk

A stream of consciousness monologue relating what happens
during a fairly typical walking meditation for the author

The most blessed part of the day,
time for a meditation walk ...   a walk with God.
My heart quickens, inwardly smiling, with exuberant anticipation of the half hour to come.

My breath quickens in mild fear of the challenges to come. It will require traveling to the edge of self-control, the outer limits of the ego bubble. Facing the void of nothingness, to reach out into God's loving bliss just beyond. Not a journey for the undisciplined, faint of heart. Nor can it be traversed without the aid of God's loving embrace.

While I pull out of the closet a pair of worn, white New Balance walking sneakers, my college-aged son exclaims "those are so old-fashioned, for old fogeys like you Dad." Laughing I think:

"Oh well, God is much older than me, so He'll probably think these are quite stylish."

I survey the outside scene, the sun is low, just before sunset, an ideal time. Most of the sidewalks and roads, will be covered in shade. The sun will not blind when looking upward. Then as the sun falls into twilight, then dusk, a calmness will descend. A descending calmness that mirrors the trajectory of my inner state and helps it along.

The path chosen is mostly straight and long, go out, turn around, return. Same path every day on this suburban, sidewalked road. With the sights having become boringly familiar, my attention more easily turns to God, an always enjoyable companion.

Out the door, onto the road ... let the walk begin.

Time: 00:00: Calm Down phase

Walking down the road at a slightly faster than normal clip, the mind reels, thoughts darting to and fro, like bumper cars endlessly colliding on a race track.

" ... tonight I need to respond to ... trash cans already out, don't forget to bring out ours ... need to go shopping later and buy ... what an awful election ... Why did they elect this man! Don't people realize what sham he is! How much damage he'll do! ... Partisan politics must be Satan's crowning achievement ... Love a Democrat! Love a Republican! Without judgement! As an equal before God! Without feeling morally superior! ... God do you really believe I am up to this task? ... Life is hard."

Need to reign in the thoughts. Stop, or at least slow down, the chattering monkey mind. Forceful suppression fails, the wild mind is too strong. Cunning tactics are required. Walk a little faster, breathe a little deeper, then deploy visual overload.

Look right ... bright pink camellias smile on a canopy of dark green leaves.

Look left ... a pair of dogs frolic as their owners converse.

Look up ... trees gently swaying in the breeze.

Thoughts melt away, the mind is overloaded with visual stimuli. Not enough computational capacity to think wild thoughts while looking and walking.

Time: 10:00: Warm Up phase

With the easy challenge secured, the most formidable challenge appears.

I could enjoy the rest of the walk normally, looking around, thinking a few but not too many, random thoughts. Then go home feeling enjoyably refreshed.

But no, the purpose of the walk is not to pleasantly revel in ego-level relaxation. No stopping before a joyful, blissful, ecstasy-filled communion with God. Or at least as close as possible this half hour.

Gently coaxing God's love in with simple devotional, love breathing. I breathe in feeling God's love enter my heart chakra, expanding it like a balloon being pumped up. Breathing out in devotional offering, I send God love through the spiritual eye chakra, while silently chanting "God" on every out-breath.

I start looking upward, feeling God's presence in the sky at my gaze point 45 degrees up. With each love breath, I feel God sending me a beam of love into my heart from the gaze point, then through my forehead I send Him back a beam of love when breathing out. It becomes a circle of love sharing, synchronized to my breath mantra "God, God, God."

While slowly shifting from looking around to just looking up, I actively start silencing random thoughts. My ego starts to go berserk with terror. The ego's operational self-identity is challenged, no visual distractions or thoughts to moor itself to, it fears extermination. An intense fight flight response activates, my heart beats faster, oxygen is short, must breathe faster deeper, an onslaught of random thoughts exponentially multiply barraging my mind, hair tingles, hands sweat.

With experience gained, I now welcome this exquisite precipice; facing an egoic abyss of retraction below and the promise of divine ecstasy above.

Will I flinch and retreat into worldly thoughts mundane?

Will I hold steadfast; gaze upheld; heart, mind, breath focused only on loving God?

As I continue down the street, step after step after step,

a startling, sudden, high-pitched squeal breaks my budding communion divine. That ultimate shredder of suburban serenity;

... a leaf blower turns on dead ahead.

"what do I do now? ... ignore with forceful discipline and walk by ... speed up and pass quickly by ... turn and take another route?"

A decision is made: "well God, this is too much of a challenge right now, I'd rather enjoy your company in quietness than exercise and strengthen my divine, disciplined will." I turn a corner to get away. Yet as I start up this new street, a child thumps a basketball ahead, a couple chatting noisily walks my way.

"Ugh! is there no escape? ... OK God, you have cornered me ... sounds in back, sounds in front ... for you God, like an Olympic athlete, I'll accept this high-intensity interval training routine, I'll walk slowly past and keep my focus only on You."

People have commented on how calm I am during conflicted, stressful encounters. This ability was developed taking love breathing walking meditations past leaf blowers!

Time 20:00 minutes: Total disciplined immersion

"just walked past the half way mark ... only have about 10 minutes till returning ... time to go all in ... total focus now"

Stand straight, chest slightly puffed forward

Head level

Eyes, motionless in their sockets,

looking up 45 degrees or more.

Time to spike the energy flow with super-charged love breathing. Now rather than accepts God's love in as a single beam of light into my heart, on each-in breath now, I feel God's love entering my body from everywhere, but mainly coming into the rear base of the head, the "mouth of God." As the energy enters in, I see it traveling down into and expanding the heart chakra. Then on the out breath, love energy flows from the spiritual eye, out upward, expanding to encompass all infinity. There at the point of exhalation, God and I together, love all, everywhere.

So much energy flows into the brain, it feels like a blood vessel might burst, especially at the temples and right above the nose. The forehead muscles start to wrinkle, too much energy bottled up there. Like a warning reminder saying "plenty of energy here to use, don't waste it on muscle contractions, expand your consciousness more, go farther out, love everywhere, to infinity unseen."

The fight flight response fully active now. My stepping pace quickens, unconsciously my body tries to physically dissipate the energy, to retract from expansion. My consciousness notices this egoic fear-based retreat tactic, I willfully slow down my pace, going slower and slower, letting the energy build more and more. Then to prevent more physical energy dissipation, I relax, still every atom of my body, like one does in Shavasana, dead man's pose. Knees become weak, wobbly. Allowing just enough energy, not one bit more, to keep them walking step by step.

Thoughts still enter, even distracting for a moment, but are more easily vanquished, simply sending them out, on the breath, up to God's purifying, vaporizing rays.

Maya and Satan panic, outwitted at every turn, they attempt their shrewdest, most insidious lure:

"so it's calmness you desire, mindfulness beyond thoughts and agitation you want, stillness you seek. I can provide ..."

My head relaxes, my heart slows, my breath calms,

Thoughts completely go,

Consciousness sinks below all egoic agitations disdained.

Entering into a silent, stupor of walking sleep

Joy fades

God is forgotten.

The triggered heartache signals me louder than any train horn blaring its warning:

"NO! NO! NO! ... this is not where I want to be! ... not

what I came to walk for!"

Refocusing on breathing out love infinite, quickly, with surprising ease, the divine communion reconnects. I feel the blood pressure in my head rise. Such a useful gauge, any lowering of blood pressure signals me to focus more completely, fix my gaze more solidly, expand my hearts love joy more widely.

In one sense, the walk becomes an exercise in maximizing the head's forward blood pressure. An obvious shallow view of such a profound practice, nevertheless it helps guide my focus.

With each step, the green-leaved trees dotting yards, slowly pass through the range of perceptual vision, going behind, out-of-sight. New ones get closer, and closer, replacing the ones behind, until they too fall behind, out-of-sight. A never-ending parade of trees on either side of the forward, upward gaze.

Power lines traverse overhead, moving across the sky blue background, up, over, disappearing behind. Clouds float left, right, and above. Housetops, treetops overlay the lower canopy of the scene above. Pedestrians and bicyclist appear ahead and besides. Small fuzzy blobs they appear. With gaze upward transfixed, no crisp outlines are revealed. Growing, growing as they approach, still blobs at standard size, until they to travel behind, out of sight.

In this exquisite state of fixated, equilibrium sustained, God and I smile together and hum across the heavens.

Home approaches, gratitude flows, while yet today the bubbling bliss did not visit, I content with this walk in the warm, loving joy of God-shared communion. Returning home, I stand outside still as a statue, looking upward transfixed for a moment. This onset of sudden stillness arouses an additional surge of peaceful, sparkling joy, which fills my body, fills the air around. I walk inside, seating myself with closed eyes, meditate in still silence of God's love embraced.

For Beginning Meditators

Walking naturally helps calm the mind, making it easier to enter a meditative state. The walk can be a meditation in itself or can be used to help one go into a sitting meditation. One beginning meditator commented to me, "I can only meditate after taking a walk."

If you are a beginning meditator, the training manual is still very useful, but with modification. I wrote the manual based on my own experience. As I had been meditating for over 15 years before starting walking meditations, some of training manual suggestions might prove too difficult for someone just starting out.

Meditation should help one become calmer, more still. Trying to force oneself into stillness more than you are ready for, will backfire, causing internal rebellion, which takes away from calm stillness.

Here are suggestions if you do use the training manual and are just starting out on a meditation practice:

- Don't try to fix your gaze at one point toward the end of a walk. Keep looking out, up, and around, not down. See and feel God in everything you see. You can start looking around slower and slower if it helps you become calmer. Adjust the amount of looking around to how much stillness you can easily endure.

- If you don't have a sitting meditation practice the walk itself can be your full practice. After the walk is over, you can also try sitting for a minute or two with your eyes open or closed while continuing to love breathe.

  While using love breathing as a sitting meditation can be done, it is not optimal. If you are interested in sitting meditations, this author suggests you learn several different ones, to see which is better for you. In particular I found the "Hong Sau" meditation taught through Ananda (ananda.org), most useful.

- A simplified love breath can be tried: feel love/energy in your heart chakra while breathing in, feel love/energy at your spiritual eye while breathing out. Disregard trying to feel a flow of love back and forth. Instead, while walking think about God, talk with God, ask God questions, share your life happenings with God.

- Many people will listen to spiritual music, spiritual talks, or recordings of uplifting affirmations while walking. These walks can be enhanced by standing straight with your chest slightly puffed out while walking. This will help open up your heart chakra. Also look out and up, not down, while walking and listening. Then if possible you can also do the simplified love breath. This should be simple enough for one to do while listening and walking, but if not, disregard this suggestion.

Affirmational Walking Meditation

Here's a wonderful walking meditation technique a friend of mine, Kamaladevi Beswick, does which has unique benefits.

She goes on about a one hour walk and repeats an affirmation while walking, a different affirmation each time. When starting the walk, she asks God what affirmation she should use. Then she listens and intuits with God one and uses it for the rest of the walk. Interestingly, just as I experience in a love breathing walk, it takes her about 10 minutes at first for the "chattering mind" to quiet down, then she can start intuiting an affirmation. Also she looks up and around at the sky while walking; "like being under a blue canopy of God."

Asking God for a new affirmation with every walk is a wonderful way to develop an intuitive rapport with God. This, I feel, is a unique benefit of this walk. I'd recommend anyone try it out, especially if you have found affirmations useful in your spiritual search.

Another book by the author:

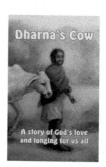

Dharna's Cow

*A story of God's love
and longing for us all*

Author's comment:

Dharna's Cow conveys the relationship, the 'courtship dance,'
between seekers of God and God. The Love Breathing Walking
Meditation helps establish such a relationship of joyous, divine
communion.

Workshops and these books are available at:

www.walkingmeditation.info

Eric Munro, a retired high-tech executive,
holds a BSEE from MIT and an MBA
from Anderson/UCLA. He resides in
Mountain View, CA while spending
his time sharing walking meditation
techniques and helping out at the Ananda
Valley Farm in Half Moon Bay, CA.

Made in USA - North Chelmsford, MA
1343398_9798848566437
11.30.2022 0819